FIRE IN THE TREETOPS

Haiku North America Anthologies

Harvest (1991)

The Shortest Distance (1993)

Northern Lights (1995)

Shades of Green (1997)

Too Busy for Spring (1999)

Paperclips (2001)

Brocade of Leaves (2003)

Tracing the Fern (2005)

Dandelion Wind (2007)

Into Our Words (2009)

Standing Still (2011)

Close to the Wind (2013)

Once Upon a Time (2015)

FIRE IN THE TREETOPS

*Celebrating Twenty-Five Years
of Haiku North America*

Michael Dylan Welch, *editor*
Christopher Patchel, *artwork*

PRESS HERE

PRESS HERE

22230 NE 28TH PLACE
SAMMAMISH, WASHINGTON
98074-6408 USA

ISBN 978-1-878798-37-4

First printing, October 2015

This book is a commemorative anthology of poems by attendees and
participants in Haiku North America conferences from 1991 through 2015,
an international celebration of haiku and related genres of poetry held
most recently at Union College in Schenectady, New York, October 14
through 18, 2015. Each attendee who chose to submit poems was
guaranteed to have one selected for inclusion in this anthology.

Design and typography by Michael Dylan Welch.
Poems set in 14/18 Nyala. Prose set in 13/18 Nyala.
Headings set in 14/18 and 26/28 Lithos Pro.

www.haikunorthamerica.com

DEDICATION

To William J. Higginson

1938 – 2008

CONTENTS

THE DEMOCRACY OF HAIKU

by Michael Dylan Welch

"We write to taste life twice,
in the moment and in retrospect."
—*Anaïs Nin*

WHERE WE'VE BEEN, WHERE WE'RE HEADED

HAIKU NORTH AMERICA began as a gathering of haiku tribes in 1991. It was the brainchild of Garry Gay, in 1990, and he carefully assembled a team of organizers who shared a vision to make this long-weekend conference as democratic as possible, welcoming all perspectives on haiku as a literary genre of poetry. It was named to embrace Canada, the United States, and Mexico, rather than being just a U.S.-centered event. The first conference took place at Las Positas College in Livermore, California, near both San Francisco and San Jose, which were homes to the Haiku Poets of Northern California and the Yuki Teikei Haiku Society. In those days, the two organizations represented a more rigid divide in their approaches to haiku than they do today, but their differences motivated HNA organizers to bring them together in the spirit of welcoming both modern and traditional approaches. HNA expanded this welcome to haiku poets across the continent to celebrate North American haiku, and conferences have received attendees and speakers from Japan, Europe, and Australasia. That first conference was, perhaps, a cotillion—a coming out of North Americans as haiku debutantes, if that hadn't already happened before. As Cor van den Heuvel said on the back cover of the first HNA conference anthology, *Harvest*, "Haiku North America is probably the most ambitious haiku event ever attempted outside of Japan. Everyone taking part in this coming-of-age celebration for English-language haiku will be helping to make literary history."

Indeed, that sense of making history has continued from conference to conference. Papers first shared at HNA soon appeared in leading haiku journals and helped to shape the landscape of North American haiku, often quoted and serving as benchmarks for haiku understanding. Initially, HNA was going to be a one-time affair, but after a year's break, the idea arose to do it again. A new team was assembled to repeat the event at Las Positas College in 1993. William J. Higginson had given the keynote address in 1991, on the democracy of haiku, and in 1993 the two keynote speakers were Jane Hirshfield and James W. Hackett.

In 1995, the conference moved to Canada for the first time, and took place at Ryerson Polytechnic University in Toronto, Ontario, in conjunction with the annual Haiku Canada meeting, attracting Martin Lucas from England, among others. In 1997, HNA migrated to Portland State University in Portland, Oregon, featuring translators Janine Beichman, Steven Carter, and Sam Hamill. Two years later, in 1999, HNA found a home at Northwestern University in Evanston, Illinois, where the keynote speaker was Gerald Vizenor, who spoke on his concept of "survivance," how Native American literature can coexist and thrive in a White society. Also appearing were Lucien Stryk, Haruo Shirane, and Robert Spiess, and the banquet featured a standout reading from Cor van den Heuvel's new edition of *The Haiku Anthology* (Norton, 1999). From the Midwest, HNA then moved to Boston, Massachusetts, where the conference was held at the Boston Conservatory in 2001. Ion Codrescu came from Romania and Hiroaki Sato made an appearance, as did Haruo Shirane. As one would expect from the conservatory location, this conference showcased many musical and dramatic interpretations of haiku.

The 2003 conference stayed on the East Coast, moving to New York City, where HNA took place at the Dalton School. Regina Weinreich spoke on Beat haiku and was part of a memorable panel discussion on the subject. HNA then moved back to the West Coast in 2005, taking place at the Fort Worden Conference Center in Port Townsend, Washington, north of Seattle. Making a special appearance was Harumi Blyth, daughter of translator R. H. Blyth, who was interviewed on stage about her famous father. HNA then moved back to the East Coast in 2007 to take place at the Hawthorne Inn and Conference Center in Winston-Salem, North Carolina. Sonia Sanchez was the keynote speaker, and HNA held its first haiku slam. John Barlow and Matthew Paul attended from England. At this conference, Tazuo Yamaguchi filmed the majority of his feature-length documentary movie, *Haiku: The Art of the Short Poem*, interviewing many haiku poets in attendance and recording their readings and presentations.

Canada hosted Haiku North America for the second time when the conference moved to Ottawa, Ontario, in 2009, at the National Library of Canada, just steps from the Parliament buildings. Keynote speakers were Robert C. Sibley and Patricia Donegan, and the Saturday-night boat cruise broke out into dancing. HNA traveled back to the West Coast in 2011, taking place at Seattle Center in Seattle, Washington, with the banquet in the iconic Space Needle, featuring a surprise appearance by Haiku Elvis (Carlos Colón). Richard Gilbert gave the first William J. Higginson Memorial Lecture, and Sunday's excursion was a boat cruise to Blake Island for a salmon bake and Native American cultural and dance performance.

The 2013 conference took place on a much larger boat. While it had long been a dream of HNA organizers to hold the conference on a cruise ship sailing to exotic ports, HNA took place aboard the Queen Mary, firmly docked in Long Beach, California. Charles Trumbull gave the Higginson lecture on hoaxes in haiku. Another highlight was the premier launch reading from Jim Kacian's newly published *Haiku in English* anthology (Norton, 2013), in addition to ghost tours of the Queen Mary and a boat trip to Catalina Island. There were also presentations on Japanese American haiku written during World War II internment camps, a first for HNA.

And now, in 2015, celebrating twenty-five years of biennial conferences, Haiku North America is at Union College in Schenectady, New York, featuring keynote addresses by Red Pine (Bill Porter) and Randy M. Brooks (with the Higginson lecture) amid fall colors at the edge of the Catskill Mountains. Ion Codrescu is the featured artist, with a gallery exhibit in Union's historic Nott Memorial Hall. HNA conferences often have themes, and the focus for 2015 is on haiku education, as its speakers and attendees look to the future and emphasize the development of new voices, both young and old, in the haiku art.

Here it is worth quoting three comments from the back cover of the 2007 HNA conference anthology, *Dandelion Wind*, for their summations of what Haiku North America had already become by then. These observations are even more true today, and will surely remain true for the future:

> "Of the small handful of regular occasions that nurture the English-language haiku community, Haiku North America is certainly preeminent: intellectually diverse, socially expansive, emotionally gratifying, it provides more than any other single experience the sense that haiku is a literary force to be reckoned with and capable of work that matters in the rest of the world." —*Jim Kacian*

"Every two years, at some interesting location in the United States or Canada, the organizers of Haiku North America put together exciting and innovative programs involving leading poets, scholars, editors, and teachers, as well as practitioners of arts that have a kinship with haiku. The result is that HNA is the most eagerly awaited conference on the haiku calendar."
—*George Swede*

"Haiku North America offers haiku poets worldwide the opportunity to renew their spirit of community. The Haiku North America conference is a remarkable setting for innovative workshops and spellbinding readings. This unique collaboration, known to its devotees as HNA, is the place to experience not only the art but also the heart of haiku."
—*Roberta Beary*

Each Haiku North America conference brings together old friends and many new voices. Traditions have developed over the years, including a banquet, a conference T-shirt, a group photo, and a memorial reading for haiku poets who have died since the previous conference. It also has a book fair, a silent auction, displays of haiga and other artwork, musical performances, the trading of trifolds or other haiku handouts, panel discussions, many readings, papers, and workshops, and of course the conference anthology, which many people try to fill with as many attendee autographs as they can. These traditions, together with surprises and changes at each conference, are part of the allure, keeping haiku poets, scholars, and translators coming back time after time.

Where Haiku North America goes in the future will be where haiku goes—wherever its poets take it. We have discussed form, debated the distinctions between haiku and senryu, and explored what is essential to haiku in English. We have pushed boundaries, yet also celebrated the middle way. We have talked about what is lost and gained in the differences between Japanese and English, as well as the cultures behind them. We have shown videos, and made them, and then discussed them. We have displayed and enjoyed haiga, traded haiku trifolds and our latest books and anthologies. We have pondered the challenges of developing seasonal references in diverse geographies. We have contemplated *gendai* haiku, visual haiku, one-line haiku. We have disagreed with each other, and often agreed, coming away with a common delight and appreciation for each other's work. But above all, as democratically as possible, we have offered our poetry to others. By becoming at least somewhat vulnerable through the act of reading, writing, and hearing our poems, we have seen what each other has seen, and felt what each other has felt. We have shared. And that's the real heart of Haiku North America.

What began as a three-day event now covers five days, and while attendance has had its ups and downs, it's lately been around 100 to 130 people, including some of the most dedicated and passionate poets writing haiku in English. Although many talented and accomplished poets have never attended HNA, the index of this anthology is a who's who of North American haiku, with an increasing number of attendees from elsewhere in the world. HNA began with a focus on North American haiku, but it has now evolved to embrace wider international audiences and concerns, even while still taking place in the United States or Canada. Perhaps HNA will one day be held in Mexico and give more attention to Hispanic haiku, or perhaps take place somewhere in the Caribbean—maybe on a cruise ship that actually cruises. Or maybe HNA could meet in Hawaii, and welcome delegates from Japanese haiku organizations in a joint event (we have, however, had a significant number of Japanese attendees through the years, such as Kazuo Sato and Emiko Miyashita, among others). Perhaps, too, HNA might garner more attention than it does from the wider poetic community, and attract more participation by poets who are not already part of the established haiku community. Whatever the case, it is certain that each conference will reflect the virtues of its host location and the tastes and goals of its organizers. And more than anything else, it will reflect current trends in haiku writing and haiku studies, celebrating new anthologies and authors, and always old friendships, continuing to welcome varied and divergent points of view in a democratic and energetic gathering of the haiku tribes.

HONORING WILLIAM J. HIGGINSON

THIS ANTHOLOGY celebrates twenty-five years of biennial Haiku North America conferences. It collects poems published in all its previous anthologies since the first conference in 1991, together with new poems for the 2015 conference. The book's title comes from one of nine poems that William J. Higginson published in anthologies from each of the first nine conferences he was able to attend before he died in 2008.

> fire in the treetops
> the truck races down the street
> trailing its hose
>
> (from *Paperclips*, 2001)

This poem is not about HNA but, as all HNA attendees know so well, it represents something of the event's frenzy—the rushing around from session to session from dawn to midnight, checking out the book fair and silent auction, meals shared here and there, and all the time spent talking with friends and acquaintances. I know that Bill himself was often up late the night before each conference revising a presentation or making other preparations. So these conferences may indeed feel like fire in the treetops, yet I also hope that, for haiku, they represent a guiding light seen from near and far. That was certainly the effect that Bill himself had on those who read his words about haiku, or heard his presentations, and it was in his memory, in 2011, that Haiku North America inaugurated the William J. Higginson Memorial Lecture series to feature a distinguished academic presentation at each conference.

My first knowledge of Bill was through his seminal book, *The Haiku Handbook* (McGraw-Hill, 1985, Kodansha International, 1989). Even three decades after its publication, it is still *the* single book I recommend to people who are interested in learning about this poetry, including its history, major practitioners, and how to write haiku in English. When I first read this book, Bill's words were those of an informed but gentle expert, and they were persuasive in expanding my understanding of haiku poetry. The same is true for countless other readers who are all in Bill's debt for his leadership, the length and breadth of his scholarly research and translations, and for his own haiku and related poetry.

Indeed, Bill was prolific not just with his writings about haiku, but with his own poetry, too. He was present at the very first meeting of the Haiku Society of America. The organization formed in 1968, when Bill was twenty-nine years old, and he was an eager and passionate contributor right from the start. He came out with his first book, a collection of Japanese haiku translations, in 1968, and his scholarship and translations would blossom thereafter. But Bill's first contributions were in the form of poems, joining and leading a growing cadre of poet-friends who were exploring haiku for the first time—and their explorations were not just firsts for themselves but often firsts by anyone writing haiku in English. Bill took a turn as HSA president in 1976 and helped focus the organization not just on reading and enjoying this poetry but on craft and aesthetics as well.

Until he died in October of 2008, Bill was the only person who had been to all nine biennial HNA conferences—at the first of which it was fitting that he gave the keynote address. Bill was nowhere more in his element than at HNA, where everyone in attendance explored the art and craft of haiku with both the head and the heart. At the tenth HNA conference in Ottawa, in the summer of 2009, Bill was afforded a special memorial, and he has been deeply missed ever since.

I first met Bill at the premier conference in 1991. I had been writing haiku for fifteen years, very badly for most of that time, but had discovered his handbook—and the Haiku Society of America—just a few years before. While he had been warm and supportive in his letters, he was even more so when we met in person. Only later when we were trusting friends would we sometimes argue over the structure or logic of a haiku essay or the politics of some tempest in the haiku teapot. He could be strident in his advice, but I grew to respect it because it was borne out of careful and deep thinking, and a valid impatience for sloppy logic or scholarship. He was eminently patient with beginners, but sometimes impatient with those more established in haiku. I believe this came from his high expectations, persistently drawing out the best from others in their haiku art.

Always by Bill's side was his wife Penny Harter—or perhaps he was always by her side. They struck me as being deeply devoted to each other. Together, for many years, even decades, they were the president and first lady of English-language haiku, and you could count on the poems or critical writing of either one of them to be valuably informed and influenced by the other. Penny softened Bill. Amid his analysis of poetry, she always reminded him of its heart. As inseparable as they always were, they each wrote with individual voices and unique styles. Like Penny, Bill also wrote longer poems, and published several books of them. Together and individually, Bill and Penny were poetically formidable, yet always remained accessible and approachable. Penny continues today, in Bill's absence, on the same shining path.

Bill also evangelized for haiku. He was not content to preach to the choir, but published numerous articles in broader poetry and educational contexts, sometimes about his beloved renku, sometimes about haiku techniques, sometimes about prominent poets from Japan who had become his friends. Likewise, his translations sought to broaden understandings and connections. In all these ways, he was both a passionate haiku ambassador and preeminent haiku role model. His anthology for children, *Wind in the Long Grass* (Simon and Schuster, 1991), is still among the best collections of haiku for children ever published, especially for its seasonal emphasis. And his books about season words in haiku, *Haiku Seasons* and *Haiku World* (both Kodansha International, 1996), are the definitive books on the subject in the English language. He was also a leading committee member for Japan's Masaoka Shiki International Haiku Award, a prestigious and generous prize that he surely would have won if he hadn't been on the selection committee. For his poetry, for his service to haiku, and for his influence on haiku writing around the world, especially in English, few can be remembered as an equal to William J. Higginson, and thus I believe he deserves respect and appreciation on par with R. H. Blyth and Harold G. Henderson.

At the 1991 HNA conference, I asked Bill to sign my haiku autograph book. He was among the very first signers. I've always asked poets to write out one or more of their favorite or best haiku—poems they wanted to be remembered by. This is the haiku Bill inscribed for me, without hesitation, at Las Positas College in Livermore, California, on August 24, 1991:

after the shower
finally able to see
this perfect rose

Indeed, haiku was Bill's "perfect rose." A year before, in one of the earliest letters he wrote to me, Bill asked for a copy of the first haiku book I published with my press. He added, "I have enjoyed your work . . . and look forward to seeing what sort of things you will do as an editor and publisher." Such simple words were enormously encouraging to a poet new to the haiku community. No doubt many other poets treasured his words to them just as passionately, and took much inspiration from them. Although haiku was Bill's perfect rose, it was not just his alone, and the very first paragraph of his *Haiku Handbook* emphasizes that the purpose of haiku is to share them.

Those of us who write haiku with enthusiasm have typically started on this path from various beginnings, each at first finding our own way. But as we travel the haiku path further and further, we quickly come to find fellow travelers taking the same route. Perhaps more than anyone else, Bill cemented that path. Yet he wasn't so vaunted as to be unapproachable and above us. Rather, he remained one of us, humbly working at his poems and criticism, including as many poets as possible in his anthologies and essays, demonstrating the democracy of haiku. He sometimes called himself a "haiku coach," and that's just what he was. Through his lectures, workshops, and extensive writings, Bill made haiku appealing and welcoming to both beginners and experienced poets. Whether at Haiku North America or at other events, or just through the printed word, Bill brought newcomers up, and kept more experienced poets and critics on their toes. His pesence at any haiku event upped everyone's game, showing us all the path of haiku. Far ahead, where the cement wasn't yet laid, Bill was one of the leaders, one of the explorers for English-language haiku. The path has become a much-loved road, and will likely become a highway, if it hasn't already. For the many people who knew and loved Bill, he was one of haiku's chief engineers. It is therefore a distinct pleasure to dedicate this anthology, in celebration of Haiku North America's twenty-fifth anniversary, to William J. Higginson. Thank you, Bill.

This Anthology

HENRY MILLER once said that "Every moment is a golden one for him who has the vision to recognize it as such." The poems that follow represent one thousand and fifty-three such moments recognized by attendees of all thirteen Haiku North America conferences over the last twenty-five years (see a complete conference list in the appendix). This collection reprints every prior anthology in its entirety, plus one supplement, and ends with poems by attendees of the 2015 conference. Each section features linocut artwork by Christopher Patchel, and also includes an appreciation of a poem selected from each conference's anthology, written by one of the organizers of that year's conference.

One may wonder, over these twenty-five years of haiku, whether the poems exhibit any changes or trends. Perhaps we see more one-line haiku, or the more subjective, conceptual, tanka-like touches of *gendai* haiku. On the other hand, some changes may not be strongly represented here even while they were going on in the haiku community beyond Haiku North America. In addition, poets have occasionally changed their names, or they've moved to a new city. Some names are missing in later anthologies because those poets had died. Some poets are beginners, and we often see their work improve if they appear again later, but some of them don't appear again at all, perhaps having changed their interests. Yet others continue to appear, sustaining their interest. One characteristic that remains constant is an abiding passion for close observation of personal experience in all its permutations. Indeed, through all the poems rings a sense of discovery, an eagerness to witness the world, to see each moment closely, and then to tell about it. This is why we write, as Anaïs Nin put it, to taste life twice—once in the moment and then in retrospect. This book collects twenty-five years of gratifying moments that we are now able to recollect in celebration.

As with the first anthology in 1991, and ever since, poems are arranged alphabetically by each poet's first name, recognizing that most of our community is still on a first-name basis. One hopes that this will always be the case—a truth that describes not just the Haiku North America community, but the larger haiku community worldwide. Locations where each poet lived at the time of publication are also included with each poem, and these locations demonstrate the geographical diversity of HNA attendees. Thank you to each poet whose work is celebrated here, to the editors and artists of each of the original anthologies, and to the writers of the haiku appreciations that close each chapter. Special thanks to all of the conference organizers and other volunteers who have made each conference not only happen but shine, giving attendees many rich memories and much to contemplate. Here's to many more years of Haiku North America, the continuing democracy of haiku, and our continuing to find—and share—these golden moments.

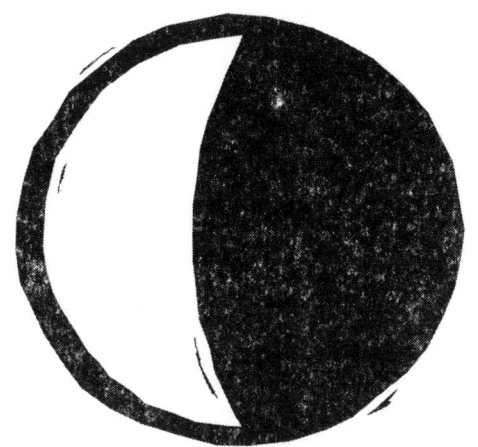

HARVEST

1991

Michael Dylan Welch, editor
August 23–25, 1991, 52 anthology contributors, one poem each

Conference Location:
Las Positas College, Livermore, California

"The haiku community on this continent is vibrant and growing, yet we are still small enough to be on a first-name basis. For this reason, the poems in this historic collection are arranged by each writer's first name." With these words from the first introduction, Haiku North America conference anthologies began a tradition of arranging the poems by each person's first name.

Dewdrops on the petals of her pink rose.

Arnold L. Langsen
Danville, California

almost touching
the harvest moon
    redwood

Art Beebe
San Jose, California

Red sun sinks and fades and cools.
Night garden breathes again
    under heaven's jewels

Beth Brewster
Livermore, California

Tall spears of dry grass
Cut and left upon the hills
Rows of golden plaid

Bun Schofield
Livermore, California

la playa blanca
mar tan turquesa
luz resplendeciente

the white beach
sea so turquoise
resplendent light

Carolanne Reynolds
West Vancouver, British Columbia

sunny beach—
    the grain of sand on my page
        has a shadow

Christopher Herold
La Honda, California

summer afternoon—
the coolness of the newspaper
from the grocery bag

Cor van den Heuvel
New York, New York

Vanity plate
on the Rolls—
"Ex-Hippie"

Dave Sutter
San Francisco, California

Crow-shriek of surprise
his withered branch falling
in an old graveyard.

Dave Wright
Pleasanton, California

shorebird feeds
with a snowflake
on its back

David Rice
Berkeley, California

bus stop in the fog . . .
   warming my knees
      with the travel section

Ebba Story
San Francisco, California

In the hot desert mountains
a sudden chill
bleached skulls near the cave.

Ester E. White
Fairfax, California

our angry whispers
till the rain begins
to clear the air

Eugenie Waldteufel
Mill Valley, California

perfumed air
of the walkway
    home

Francine Porad
Mercer Island, Washington

Poison oak
along the unmarked trail . . .
lost again

Garry Gay
Windsor, California

Small lizard's push-ups
"he's doing it to the rock!"
tour group fourth grader

George Knox
Riverside, California

Fog shrouded sea
horizon and infinity
blend into one

Hank Dunlap
Prescott, Arizona

children in bed—
  the silent blinking
    of fireflies

Helen J. Sherry
San Diego, California

Aspen gold shimmers
Silent evergreen
Shortened days rush by

Jade Lily
San Rafael, California

Hairy Maiden Fern
sticking out of the hillside
slurping lush rain

Jane A. Harris
Comptche, California

across bamboo
the moon hangs a scroll
upon the wall

Jennifer Brutschy
Dublin, California

lottery tickets
on the parking lot pavement
in the blazing sun

Jerry Ball
Livermore, California

through open windows
of my parents' empty house,
the auctioneer's song

Jerry Kilbride
San Francisco, California

Magnolia blossoms'
Arrival, two months delayed
By winter's dawdling.

John Schipper
Palo Alto, California

autumn wind—
the dry seeds rattle
   in their pods

John Thompson
Alameda, California

water skaters here
as on my childhood farm pond
the spaces between them

June Hopper Hymas
San Jose, California

home for the aged:
the century plant
in bloom

Kenneth C. Leibman
Archer, Florida

darkening sky—
my favorite umbrella
with a broken handle

Kimberly Cortner
Stockton, California

Turning the page
of a summer who-dun-it
—leaving a chocolate fingerprint.

K. Middleton
Sacramento, California

on the back
of her motorbike
hydrangea in a pot

Kris Kondō
Kanagawa, Japan

dawn—
slowly in my room
the white chrysanthemum

Kristen Deming
Tokyo, Japan

spaghetti steaming
in the shattered bowl
earthquake

Marianne Monaco
San Francisco, California

after the story
the children still listening . . .
sounds in the wind

Marlina Rinzen
Berkeley, California

sunset

birdsong

over

and

over

the dirt road

Marshall Hryciuk
Toronto, Ontario

a tired cowboy
wrestles down the calf—
changing the diaper

Marty Steyer
Austin, Texas

ferry dock:
gulls circling
the rainbow slick

Mary Fran Meer
Bellevue, Washington

between trains
between sunset and afterglow—
nothing between us

Mary L. Hill
Palo Alto, California

old folks' home—
the square of light
crosses the room

Michael Dylan Welch
Foster City, California

an Alaskan goose
in a California pond
honks at traffic

M. L. Harrison Mackie
Comptche, California

maternity nurses
avoiding the far labor room—
    miscarriage

Pamela Connor
Clarks Green, Pennsylvania

Alone tonight—
a cricket
in the fold of my nightgown.

Patricia Donegan
San Francisco, California

the winter rains—late:
I crack the patio door
    to listen, listen

Patricia Machmiller
San Jose, California

Gathering the gold
of fallen persimmon leaves
    senior citizens

Pat Shelley
Saratoga, California

bullfrogs
answer each other
and my stomach

Paul O. Williams
Belmont, California

Japanese garden—
bamboo leaf shadows sweeping
the cobblestone walk

Rengé / David Priebe
Los Angeles, California

One falling leaf
lightly breaks the dark stillness
of early morning.

Robert Mitchell
Fremont, California

the old dog
leaves his warm bed
can opener sound

Ronan
Eugene, Oregon

In the dark morning
    suddenly a cardinal
        lights up the linden

Sue Stapleton Tkach
Rochester, New York

dark trees
emerging
poorwill poorwill poorwill

Tom Lynch
Oakland, California

Ordering
a pretzel plain
—salt on the change.

Vincent Tripi
San Francisco, California

the city boy
is the only one listening—
the song of the frogs

William J. Higginson
Santa Fe, New Mexico

through trees
hiding the ocean
sea lions bark

Winona Baker
Nanaimo, British Columbia

A Gleaning

by Jerry Ball

Harvest, the first Haiku North America conference anthology, has many striking poems, so choosing one to discuss is a difficult task. After much hesitation, however, I chose this poem by Ebba Story:

> bus stop in the fog . . .
> warming my knees
> with the travel section

Waiting at a bus stop is not new to me. I grew up in San Francisco, California, where Ebba lives, and have traveled often on the city's bus system. The season word in this haiku is "fog," indicating autumn or winter in San Francisco. Cold and lonely.

I like this verse probably because of my history of being involved with the San Francisco municipal transportation system, but I also like the poem for other reasons. First, the poem surprises us. How often might we warm our knees with the newspaper's *travel* section? Consider if we had warmed our knees with the sports section. How would that affect our response to the haiku? I am at a bus stop, traveling, and use the travel section to warm my knees. This is a pleasant surprise. So I'm traveling in more ways than one.

Second, what about technical details, the haiku's language and structure? The words are rich, clear, and concise. No extra words are tacked on to suit some future reader's tastes. Less is more. The poem has just enough words to get the job done and no more.

What about the bigger picture? Haiku is sometimes said to show just the tip of the iceberg. The spiritual content is hidden, somehow to be mined by readers. Consider the loneliness of this travel moment. If you've spent time at a big-city bus stop, you will understand this feeling of isolation. Yet we may smile, too, at being cold while wanting to be somewhere warmer, discovering that the place we are dreaming of is warming us in an unexpected way. Even if we can't get there by bus, at least the newspaper's travel section is providing physical solace.

The newspaper provides spiritual solace, too. Some people ask whether haiku is a spiritual teacher or simply a slogan. In this poem, Ebba is a spiritual teacher. We learn from things as they truly are, not from what they're advertised to be. Indeed, we are not really warmed by the idea of exotic travel but by the physical reality of the newspaper itself, as best as it can manage. The imagery is concrete, and functions as an objective correlative to the source of surprise. The point is shown, not told.

I believe Ebba's haiku succeeds on many counts, and I'm happy to travel with her in her warming poem.

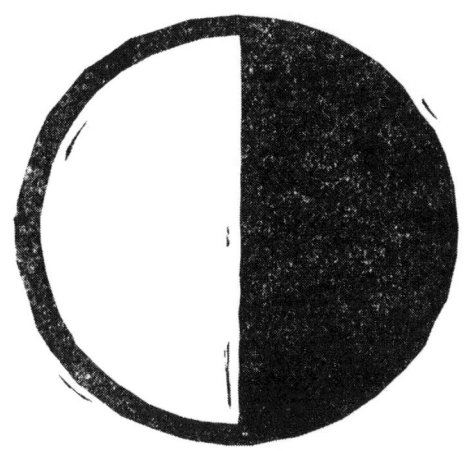

THE SHORTEST DISTANCE

1993

Ebba Story and Michael Dylan Welch, editors
Garry Gay, cover photograph

July 15–18, 1993, 51 anthology contributors,
plus 22 contributors in the supplement, one poem each

Conference Location:
Las Positas College, Livermore, California

"We are normally separated by spatial and temporal distance. As we gather to share and celebrate our involvement with haiku, that distance dissolves. We are drawn together over the shortest distance—shorter even than the written forms we cherish. We meet in the moment where hearts and minds open and rejoice. There is no distance here."
—*from the introduction*

shallow pool
littered with camellias—
a turtle, asleep

Alex Benedict
Los Gatos, California

wind-turned leaves
of the young olive tree;
silver, green, silver

Alice Benedict
Los Gatos, California

moonrise
outside the hospital
nurses take a drag

Barry Goodmann
Hackensack, New Jersey

Booming of the surf,
Ancient elemental rhythms . . .
    Salt taste on my lips.

> *Beth Brewster*
> *Livermore, California*

standing above the creek
staring down into it
the young cow

> *Bruce Ross*
> *Rochester, New York*

at summer sunrise
a mockingbird greets the day
with a borrowed song

> *Bun Schofield*
> *Livermore, California*

Hoeing the rows
    shoes hurt
        corn on little toe

> *Charlene Villella*
> *Pleasanton, California*

half-closed eyes . . .
one lash draws a beam
    from the candle

        Christopher Herold
        Woodside, California

lonely night
the faces painted on the window
of a toy bus

        Cor van den Heuvel
        New York, New York

Horse trailer:
one tail in,
one tail out

        Dave Sutter
        San Francisco, California

Spread before the sea
on a flat escarpment
a thousand pumpkins

        Dave Wright
        Pleasanton, California

blowing east
chimney smoke and my breath—
sun rises

David Rice
Berkeley, California

Practicing T'ai Chi
on the porch . . .
knowing which boards shift

Donna D. Gallagher
Sunnyvale, California

and this eclipse
    circled on my calendar
rain dots the window

Ebba Story
San Francisco, California

At my approach
the green chameleon jumps
    from the fence to the hedge

Elizabeth Nichols
Colorado Springs, Colorado

american flag
edges shredded
all the way back to the stars

Eugenie Waldteufel
Mill Valley, California

dusty town
a row of U-Haul trucks
on Main Street

Francine Porad
Mercer Island, Washington

Antique map;
an ant travels
the old spice route

Garry Gay
Windsor, California

casket lowering . . .
cemetery ground squirrels
vanish in their holes

George Knox
Riverside, California

my face deep
in white lilac
I hear no bees

Geraldine C. Little
Mt. Holly, New Jersey

frost-sharp stars
prick the purple darkness
—pond ice snaps

Hank Dunlap
Prescott, Arizona

against the blue sky
a silhouetted blackbird—
someone whistles

Helen J. Sherry
San Diego, California

through dry pines
wind makes the sound of
flowering water

J. Ervin
Colstrip, Montana

in the attic
the lonely child
hugs grandma's dress form

Jean Dubois
Golden, Colorado

sunset shadows
the curve of the swan's neck
as she settles

Jean Jorgensen
Edmonton, Alberta

a stand of iris
the sudden turn of the koi
raises the bottom

Jerry Ball
Livermore, California

leg in a cast
   watching the clock's pendulum
      swing to and fro

                    Jerry Kilbride
                    San Francisco, California

   twilight bather
bending low over the river
   slender-leafed willow

                    John Thompson
                    Santa Rosa, California

the precise placement
of blackbirds along a wire
      —early winter

                    June Hopper Hymas
                    San Jose, California

inside the dark privy
above the door frame
snake eyes

Kay F. Anderson
Redwood City, California

starched white uniforms
in the polished corridors
our footsteps echo

K. Middleton
Sacramento, California

Yangtze river
flowing still and deep—
cicadas crying

Kenichi Sato
Sakata, Japan

Watermelon Queen . . .
the faces of the contestants
in the county paper

Kenneth C. Leibman
Archer, Florida

the woman
who never married
plants forget-me-nots

Kenneth Tanemura
Redwood City, California

something in the moon
makes me want to pick
wild mushrooms

Lequita Vance
Carmel, California

Blackberry brambles;
covey of ptarmigans
hidden by snowfall

Lorraine Ellis Harr / Tombo
Portland, Oregon

wind blows through the cracks
and then out again
sitting zazen

Margaret Chula
Portland, Oregon

under desert stars
      cactus
strung with lights

Marianne Monaco
San Francisco, California

low summer sun—
the shadow of an earring
on your cheek

Michael Dylan Welch
Foster City, California

One prostitute
one snail
along O'Farrell Street

Pat Donegan
San Francisco, California

Pine needles falling
to the dry forest floor
one on another

Pat Shelley
Saratoga, California

sitting down to think
suddenly through my Levis
chill of the stone bench

Patricia Machmiller
San Jose, California

past midnight
another acorn
whacks the truck hood

Paul O. Williams
Belmont, California

down from the mountain
the tourist fingers
a lump of lava

Penny Harter
Santa Fe, New Mexico

Pile of weeded vines
moldering more than a week . . .
morning-glory blooms!

Rengé / David Priebe
Los Angeles, California

fishing poles in hand
stepping off the bus
father and daughter

Robert Epstein
Berkeley, California

Starting the shower
I bow my apologies
to the spider.

Sherryl Smith
Santa Barbara, California

my son's toes
dipped in the sea—
his grip tightens

Tom Lynch
Martinez, California

the fence post
hangs upright in the washout—
mid-summer heat

William J. Higginson
Santa Fe, New Mexico

rock garden—
a fallen camellia floats
in the sea of gravel

Yoko Ogino
Kobe, Japan

frosty morning
    my black cat taking up
the one patch of sun

Yvonne Hardenbrook
Murrysville, Pennsylvania

HAIKU NORTH AMERICA 1993 SUPPLEMENT

The following twenty-two poems were collected for a supplement to the 1993 HNA anthology by Carolanne Reynolds, with assistance from George Pajari. These poets, each with a poem they selected themselves, had not submitted for the regular conference anthology, which was printed before the conference began. Unlike all other anthology submissions, a few of these poems have been published previously.

summer squall
singing the skin
smiling the face

Arthur Lev-Abrams
Carlsbad, California

silver anniversary
awake with the midnight moon
—cut lavender

B. H. Feingold
Berkeley, California

It's raining again . . .
out   come   umbrellas
Vancouver's winter flowers

Carolanne Reynolds
West Vancouver, British Columbia

waiting in darkness . . .
    an aged blind man sitting,
        listening for the moon

> *Chris Thorsen*
> *Mill Valley, California*

Redtop Mountain Road
Covered by the drifting snow
Prints of cloven hoof

> *Edward Sherry*
> *San Diego, California*

        starling flying past
the entrance—automatic
            doors   open

> *George Klacsanzky*
> *Edmonds, Washington*

haiku poet
        waiting for inspiration
no frog jumps to mind

> *George Pajari*
> *West Vancouver, British Columbia*

dozing by the waterfall . . .
a frog too
with one eye open
like me

George Swede
Toronto, Ontario

rekindled feelings
deep within illuminate
my beginner's mind

Hank Grum
Livermore, California

On nearing the surf
every footprint becomes
that of the sea

James W. Hackett
La Honda, California

hills
touching each other
at the river

Jane Reichhold
Gualala, California

against the brick wall
three shadows
and the red ball

Jeffrey Winke
Milwaukee, Wisconsin

haiku poetry
three lines, few syllables
fast food for thought

John Schipper
Palo Alto, California

The smile on her lips
relieves tension between us
pitch dark sunglasses

Kiyoko Tokutomi
San Jose, California

Autumn deepening—
the voices of insects
polish the moon

Kristen Deming
Bethesda, Maryland

cycles déjà vu
    alpha and the omega
        reborn into death

Louise L. Birk
San Francisco, California

mist shadows
    a white heron perched
above the river

Marshall Hryciuk
Toronto, Ontario

the hungry man
   leaves a perfect orange
      on the altar

Mary Rudge
Alameda, California

mother and daughter
weave together on the loom
        mist around the house

Nick Avis
Cornerbrook, Newfoundland

a nightmare—
it takes a while for the frogs
to sing again

Randy Johnson
Olympia, Washington

black clouds gathering
we align the living room
        buckets

Virginia Haddad
Tujunga, California

Sleeping wind
in the oval of an egg
    already wings

Werner Reichhold
Gualala, California

DISCOVERY

by Garry Gay

my son's toes
dipped in the sea—
his grip tightens

In all the best haiku, there is more to meet the eye than on first reading, and this haiku by Tom Lynch, then living in Martinez, California, is no exception. Under the surface lies a mixture of emotions that captivates us. The poem paints a beautiful image in our minds. It also opens up questions. For example, is this the child's first time visiting the ocean? If so, then what a thrilling experience it has to be for a young mind to take in all of the sea's vastness. Yet perhaps all he can take in is the wave in front of him, that first dip in the water at his toes, and maybe the rest of the ocean is too much to think about.

We can sense both excitement and fear when we read that the boy's grip tightens. After his moment of fear, I am sure he will relax, let go, and want to run and splash through the cool water. Yet even the smallest shore waves push against his small body, so he tightens his grip, trusting his father's safety. It's fun for children—and adults—to feel the pull of the sea as each wave retreats, our toes being sucked into the wet sand, and surely the boy will soon be enjoying just that. This poem does what every finely written haiku should do—it takes you back to one of your own experiences when you were young. Tom's poem is full of childhood memories.

But that's not all. The poem also tells the story of the father, who is introducing his son to the sea while making sure he feels safe. The father may think the ocean is a fun and inviting place for his son to play, yet when the boy's grip tightens, the father suddenly realizes that his son is afraid. It's a fleeting moment, shared between a man and a boy, perhaps like many moments to come as the boy learns to discover his world.

Above all, Tom Lynch's poem brims with the feeling of being alive, experiencing the adventure of that first time on an expansive seashore. Perhaps this sense of wonder, this same sense of discovery, is present in all haiku, and we might read each poem we ever read as if we were experiencing it for the very first time.

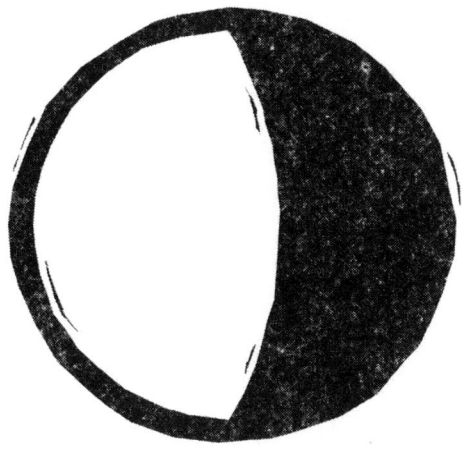

Northern Lights

1995

Michael Dylan Welch, editor

July 13–15, 1995, 51 poems by 30 anthology contributors,

one or two poems each

Conference Location:

Ryerson Polytechnic University, Toronto, Ontario

With the 1995 conference, Haiku North America visited Canada for the first time. This conference's anthology is divided into two sections, the first with more of a view towards nature and the seasons, titled "Northern Lights," the second with more of a focus on senryu, titled "Northern *Lights.*" Unlike most HNA conference anthologies, this one was published after the conference. "Whether you are the lone haiku voice in an isolated town, or one of many talented poets in a single city enjoying much camaraderie, haiku is its own reward." *—from the introduction*

Northern Lights

spring breeze—
some of the seedlings turn over
in the road

Bruce Ross
Rochester, New York

Spirit wood
Buddha's children—moist young buds
on long thin branches

David Michaels
North York, Ontario

Candlelit night
   only one moth
      finds the source

Elizabeth Warren
Owen Sound, Ontario

view windows
behind the guest speaker
wind twists the leaves

Francine Porad
Mercer Island, Washington

Weeping willows:
branches droop yet upright trees
tower over roofs.

Frances Mary Bishop
Toronto, Ontario

The river forks . . .
our raft drifts
through summer clouds

Garry Gay
Windsor, California

sss-pit, sss-pit
goes the sprinkler
among the cherry trees

George Swede
Toronto, Ontario

Morning garbage truck
taking bottles, boxes, cans . . .
leaving the quiet

Gerald St. Maur
Toronto, Ontario

twilight
a descending 747
sets off a car alarm

Hans Jongman
Weston, Ontario

autumn sunset—
a berry between the toes
of a titmouse

Jeff Witkin
Potomac, Maryland

broken umbrella
keeping a patch of sidewalk
wet

John Bergstrom
Boston, Massachusetts

in March sunshine—
socks still frozen on the line

Judith Anderson Stuart
Mississauga, Ontario

barefoot in wet grass
the soft bursting
of the slug

Karen Sohne
Amityville, New York

country road . . .
slanted sunbeams following
the pickup truck

Kenneth C. Leibman
Archer, Florida

into the field
   of fallen leaves
      warmth on my feet

Kim Horne
St. Catherines, Ontario

dusk at winter's end
the cardinal's color
goes into its song

LeRoy Gorman
Napanee, Ontario

mist in the canyon
skimming the river
my kayak and I

Louise Beaven
Toronto, Ontario

after the grand opening
of the new city hall
a deflated balloon

Margaret Saunders
Hamilton, Ontario

cool sunset—
on the footpath
a punctured balloon

Martin Lucas
Lancaster, England

red admiral

darts out

over the shed

Marshall Hryciuk
Toronto, Ontario

Hanukkah candles
faint scent of mothballs from the
hand-women prayer shawl

Muriel Ford
Toronto, Ontario

cedar waxwings
in the hawthorn tree
red berry stains on the snow

Patricia Neubauer
Allentown, Pennsylvania

still the hawk
circles over this summer's
housing development

Penny Harter
Santa Fe, New Mexico

blackbird on the light standard
shakes out the wind—
homeless man sleeps

Raffael de Gruttola
Natick, Massachusetts

night walk—
stars
in the pine branches

Sarah Jensen
Boston, Massachusetts

still awake
my thoughts drifting
with the stars

Suezan Aikins
Prospect, Nova Scotia

steam rising
after the snow squall:
buds on the lilac

Timothy Russell
Toronto, Ohio

summer solstice
the cat wakes up
a few minutes early

William J. Higginson
Santa Fe, New Mexico

parade over
old vet stumbles down the street—
poppies in the gutter

Winona Baker
Nanaimo, British Columbia

Northern Lights . . .

so vast now
the old cow pasture filled
with deep spring grass

Bruce Ross
Rochester, New York

Country girl asks,
    "are there blood-suckers
        in this pool?"

Elizabeth Warren
Owen Sound, Ontario

haiku presenter
foolishly suggests
we close our eyes

Francine Porad
Mercer Island, Washington

The last tea bag
used
for the fifth time

Garry Gay
Windsor, California

As the bald poet reads
a spot of light dances from
hemisphere to hemisphere

George Swede
Toronto, Ontario

ignored completely
at the dinner party
a moose on the wall

Jeff Witkin
Potomac, Maryland

behind the speaker—
maples leaves shake in the wind

John Bergstrom
Boston, Massachusetts

too many flies—
we picnic inside

Judith Anderson Stuart
Mississauga, Ontario

the moon in a gap in fast moving clouds

Karen Sohne
Amityville, New York

dark at last . . .
the first skyrocket bursts
our conversation

Kenneth C. Leibman
Archer, Florida

bIrDsCrOwDtOsPlAsHiNtHeSaMePuDdLe

LeRoy Gorman
Napanee, Ontario

in the pine-scented air
sniffing the aroma
of barbequed steak

Louise Beaven
Toronto, Ontario

at the haiku workshop
everyone an expert

Margaret Saunders
Hamilton, Ontario

lovemaking
the sash windows
rattle

Martin Lucas
Lancaster, England

imported art exhibit
the twittering
            of tape machines

Marshall Hryciuk
Toronto, Ontario

with mist burned off
surrounded by lavender
    I hum with the bees

Muriel Ford
Toronto, Ontario

first ballet class—
new tights wrinkling
on little stick legs

Patricia Neubauer
Allentown, Pennsylvania

almost finished
with the romance novel—
high tide

Penny Harter
Santa Fe, New Mexico

tumbling
from the blue envelope
red
    gold
        leaves from home

Sarah Jensen
Boston, Massachusetts

smiling
he sprinkles pollen
on her belly

Suezan Aikins
Prospect, Nova Scotia

    the full moon
in the summer pond . . .
    upside down

Timothy Russell
Toronto, Ohio

a dark path
across the lawn
ends in a snowman

Winona Baker
Nanaimo, British Columbia

LEFT BEHIND

by Marshall Hryciuk

The third Haiku North America conference took place at Ryerson Polytechnic University in Toronto, Ontario in July of 1995. In *Northern Lights*, the conference anthology, I especially enjoyed the following haiku by John Bergstrom from Boston, Massachusetts:

> broken umbrella
> keeping a patch of sidewalk
> wet

Three reasons why I like this poem are that it offers a direct statement of the uncreated being equal to the natural, it employs direct diction, and it has appropriate vowel harmony.

First, something breaks. It is discarded from the human milieu and reenters the natural realm. But it still has physical effects on its natural surroundings. Human self-centeredness is trumped. Life goes on whether humans are there or not, whether humans like what happens or not. The umbrella is left behind because it's considered useless in its human-dedicated function—and now it preserves a chiaroscuro effect on the sidewalk. The bliss of no subject-object duality.

Second, it's direct. The first line has no articles. What is there is what is written and it is clear: modifier, noun. The next line shows continuing action. The third line provides a one-syllable conclusion. Dramatic, final. We see accomplished writing of a transcendent fact completed.

And third, the soft "e" sounds of "en" and "el" (I'd prefer to call them closed) in the first line are reiterated in a standalone phoneme of the last line, "wet." This is pleasing enough, but to have the long "e" of "keep" echoed by the "ing" (which is really an "ee" sound) in the second line between them for vocular juxtaposition is wonderful. So, too, is having three open vowels, each with four closed vowels between them. A most enjoyable haiku.

Shades of Green

1997

Michael Dylan Welch, editor
Cherie Hunter Day, illustration

July 24–27, 1997, 63 anthology contributors, one poem each

Conference Location:
Portland State University, Portland, Oregon

haiku conference
someone clears a frog
from his throat

Yvonne Hardenbrook
Columbus, Ohio

"Haiku poets are universally attuned to nature, whether that nature is a glacial moraine, a piece of redwood bark, dolphins in the sun-sparkled ocean, or a humble window planter shadowed by clouds between skyscrapers. We notice the weather, the light, the temperature, the bird songs that ebb and flow with the seasons. Our haiku are also about each other, and about ourselves. We are attuned to human nature, noticing and celebrating the subtleties of our passing emotions, imperfections, and interaction with nature. Knowing nature—and human nature—sustains us." —*from the introduction, including the poem by Yvonne Hardenbrook*

litter
and a few fallen leaves
gather in the gutter

Alex Benedict
San Francisco, California

leafless birches
whiten the twilight path
along the streambank

Alice Benedict
San Francisco, California

Rare spring wildflowers
growing in a neighbor's grass
sound of a lawn mower

Bette R. Jones
Merritt Island, Florida

abandoned ranch house
bales of fresh hay
stacked in the yard

Brad Wolthers
Hillsboro, Oregon

off a tall building
I drop
your name

Carlos Colón
Shreveport, Louisiana

spring cleaning . . .
behind a trash-laden couple
their sauntering dogs

Carol Conti-Entin
Shaker Heights, Ohio

rising mist—
flood waters reach
another slat in the fence

Ce Rosenow
Portland, Oregon

outside the window—
a mockingbird sings all night
with cricket basso

Cherie Garvin-Jameison
Portland, Oregon

a visit with my father . . .
beneath an outdoor spigot
the tall grass

Cherie Hunter Day
Portland, Oregon

window frost
    our names drip
    from my finger

Christopher Herold
Redwood City, California

spring thaw
in a quiet part of the park
water drips into a drain

Cor van den Heuvel
New York, New York

alone and so round
in deepening night, the moon
from paper to pearl

Connie Hutchison
Kirkland, Washington

midday heat
in the charred forest
thin shadows

D. Claire Gallagher
Sunnyvale, California

104

one drop   then two
from our tent we watch
circles in the lake

Doris H. Thurston
Port Townsend, Washington

The hush before dawn:
everything waits for something
to happen

D. W. Parry
Lake Oswego, Oregon

a fox in the dunes . . .
our hushed whispers
in the autumn mist

Ebba Story
San Francisco, California

"I can't hear you,"
he says, continuing to
munch potato chips . . .

Elizabeth Nichols
Colorado Springs, Colorado

fluffy dandelion seeds
escaping from his pocket
into fluorescent light

Emiko Miyashita
Miyamae-ku, Kawasaki, Japan

Dawn
mosquito and I
ready for breakfast

E. Robert Sinnett
Manhattan, Kansas

reflected
in a beggar's cup
tropical sun

Fay Aoyagi
San Francisco, California

heavy snowfall
the last bus leaves
in chains

Francine Porad
Mercer Island, Washington

My traveling hat—
another heron feather
added to the brim

Garry Gay
Windsor, California

music—
to erase the tune
in my head

Grace Hull
Chambersburg, Pennsylvania

silent bells
a swallow swoops
to its noisy nest

Helen J. Sherry
San Diego, California

late at night
our neighbor waltzes past her window
cradling a cat

Helen K. Davie
Atascadero, California

she promised to meet me
    at the movie theatre
where part of me still waits

James Tipton
Glade Park, Colorado

ちる花にもつるゝ鳥の翼かな
chiru hana ni motsururu tori no tsubasa kana

Shiki

entangled with
the scattering cherry blossoms—
the wings of birds!

Janine Beichman, translator
Tsukuba-shi, Ibaraki-ken, Japan

in the dark . . .
we drive past a meadow
of new-mown hay

Jean Jorgensen
Edmonton, Alberta

leaning heavily
on a borrowed walking stick
the day grows longer

Jerry Ball
Seal Beach, California

climbing the fence
to join the captives
toddler at the zoo

John Schipper
Palo Alto, California

Voice and music
float over the sea of rocks
Japanese garden

Joyce M. Leonard
Milwaukie, Oregon

On Highway 24 today
I had to take myself to task
for sunflower gazing.

Kathleen K. Sinnett
Manhattan, Kansas

against a night sky
the mountain range faint
the first snow

Kenichi Sato
Sakata, Yamagata, Japan

deserted beach—
driftwood's dull sheen
in the thick fog

Kevin Hull
Atascadero, California

she leans
on the porch rail
far off mountains

Kim Hodges
Kennewick, Washington

rubber boots
upside down on stakes
the ends of tomato rows

Kris Kondō
Atsugi, Kanagawa, Japan

a blanket across us—
watching the earth's shadow
    cover the moon

Laurie W. Stoelting
Mill Valley, California

forget-me-not—
I forgot
how blue they are

Lidia Rozmus
Vernon Hills, Illinois

tangled sheets . . .
a robin
sings outside our window

Marc Thompson
Seattle, Washington

the morning after—
cutting only the orchids
flattened by rain

Margaret Chula
Portland, Oregon

rain-soaked
 newspaper
microwaved

Mary Fran Meer
Bellevue, Washington

landing swallow—
the ship's chain
dips slightly

Michael Dylan Welch
Foster City, California

the womanly smell
of the forest floor—
morels pushing through

Nasira Alma
Portland, Oregon

December rain—
still blooming
two pink rosebuds

Pamela Miller Ness
New York, New York

Christmas dinner
a flock of chickadees
in the forsythia

Pat Gallagher
Sunnyvale, California

maple leaves
barely moving
in the earthquake

Patricia Donegan
Nakano-ku, Tokyo, Japan

digging a grave
for the family dog
his old bone

paulmorin
Portland, Oregon

phone call
from a faraway friend—
the cat starts purring

Penny Harter
Santa Fe, New Mexico

Summer solstice
and everywhere blossoming
umbrellas

Peter Kendall
Portland, Oregon

deepening twilight—
   my wife turns on
   a small lamp

Rich Youmans
North Falmouth, Massachusetts

blue shadows of dusk
boy and blue heron
in the shallows

Rita Zangar Mazur
Richland, Washington

A red dragonfly . . .
off in a new direction
with each breath of wind

Robert Major
Poulsbo, Washington

compassionate words
of the old friend's eulogy—
billowing incense

Roger Abe
Morgan Hill, California

summer camp night
empty boats at the dock
moon rocking

Ronan
Eugene, Oregon

trimmed in gold
beneath the autumn aspens
this small blue spruce

Ruth Holter
Eugene, Oregon

晦日月なし千歳の杉を抱く嵐

misoka tsuki nashi chitose no sugi o daku arashi

Bashō

The month's last night, moonless—
a thousand-year-old cedar
embraced by the wind

Sam Hamill, translator
Port Townsend, Washington

緑にも色様々や雨の庭

midori ni mo iro samazama ya ame no niwa

All the same green, yes,
but how many different shades there are!
Garden in the rain.

Steven Carter
Irvine, California

Midnight stillness
just a pattering
on the young leaves

Tombo / Lorraine Ellis Harr
Portland, Oregon

through blossom light
into the gathering dusk
the swift bus

William J. Higginson
Santa Fe, New Mexico

Two months of rain.
Today,
a shadow.

Winnifred Jaeger
Kirkland, Washington

Summer afternoons
with Koreans and Arabs
    Lessons in the park

> *Woodson Taylor*
> *Englewood, Colorado*

the bell
reverberates—
fluttering petals

> *Yoshie Ishibashi*
> *Nakano-ku, Tokyo, Japan*

bay in fog
    the sailboat at anchor
comes and goes

> *Yvonne Hardenbrook*
> *Columbus, Ohio*

COMING AND GOING

by Ce Rosenow

bay in fog
    the sailboat at anchor
comes and goes

This poem is by Yvonne Hardenbrook, of Columbus, Ohio. It conveys a moment in which two things happen simultaneously and, when experienced together, convey the connectedness of things. We see fog on the bay, and a sailboat. The sailboat is visible or invisible depending on the density of the fog around it. Connectedness.

The poem's second line also functions as a pivot so that the reader experiences a new awareness when reading the third line. Because the second line concludes with "at anchor," the reader does not anticipate that the sailboat "comes and goes" and is thereby surprised in the third line.

This haiku also involves more than one of the senses. In this poem about what is seen and not seen, the primary sense is visual, but fog also has a tactile quality. The reader can feel the fog's coolness and moisture. The reference to the bay also enables us to smell the salt water. Using images that involve multiple senses gives the reader a stronger experience of the haiku moment.

Furthermore, Hardenbrook structures her lines so that they formally mirror the action taking place in the poem. Just as the sailboat comes and goes, the second line moves out away from the left margin. The third line returns back to the margin so that it is aligned with the first line of the poem. The words, too, come and go.

This haiku reminds us that our perceptions affect the way we understand things. The sailboat does not really come and go in terms of its location on the water. Hardenbrook relies on the reader's recognition of this reality to give the third line more impact. The sailboat is at anchor and we do not expect it to come and go. After that surprise, we realize that it is the boat's visibility that comes and goes because of the fog.

The poem presents further realizations because the moment incorporates elements of nature and the human experience. The image of the bay in fog creates a natural setting. The fog literally comes and goes in degrees of density, which is why the sailboat appears and disappears. The sailboat, however, is a human creation. The poem suggests metaphorically that humans, just as their creations, come and go. Transience is central to the natural world and to human experience, which emphasizes the connectedness of things. Transience is conveyed well in Hardenbrook's haiku.

Too Busy for Spring

1999

Michael Dylan Welch and Lee Gurga, editors
Lidia Rozmus, cover illustration

July 8–11, 1999, 91 anthology contributors, one poem each

Conference Location:
Northwestern University, Evanston, Illinois

"One poem or another within this book's pages will likely stop you with a spark of recognition. That's how a good haiku works—it captures the essence of a particular moment in such a way that you see what the poet saw, and feel what the poet felt. In its steadfast focus on the particular, a haiku moves us by its clear report of suchness. We see the way sunlight glances off a watch crystal, and we are fascinated like a cat that tries to catch the light. In response to a successful haiku we laugh, we cry, we nod our heads. The best part is that the words don't get in the way. In a good haiku we see what caused the poet's emotional response, not the response itself. Thus we can have the same intuitive reaction ourselves." —*from the introduction*

rain turning to snow—
the cat's tail
flicks sharply

A. C. Missias
Philadelphia, Pennsylvania

in the schoolyard
one of the saplings
has failed to bloom

Alan Pizzarelli
Bayonne, New Jersey

fish ladder
a lone salmon gazes out
the observation window

Anita Krumins
Toronto, Ontario

months after Christmas
this pine needle
in my foot

Bennett Rader
Plymouth, Ohio

dusk
   on the rocking chair
   unfinished sweater

Betty Kaplan
Adventura, Florida

camellias in bloom
visiting neighbors
until my socks grow wet

Brett B. Bodemer
Seattle, Washington

night drive
radio station fading
before the symphony's end

Bruce Detrick
New York, New York

Valentine's day
heart candy
in the condom bowl

Bruce England
Sunnyvale, California

lake breeze—
the mating dragonflies
coast backwards

Bruce Ross
Burlington, Vermont

rookie's first hit—
picked off at first

Bud Goodrich
Winnetka, Illinois

closing arguments—
the length of the lawyer's
skirt

Carlos Colón
Shreveport, Louisiana

a week till the road trip—
the old suitcase
half-packed

Charles Rossiter
Oak Park, Illinois

sure, I have my thoughts
about his body piercings,
but I bite my tongue

Charles Trumbull
Evanston, Illinois

stamping them
    the children are enjoying
    cherry blossoms

Christopher Herold
Port Townsend, Washington

morning light
through the lake-shore pines
a distant crow

Cor van den Heuvel
New York, New York

playground at dusk . . .
back and forth on the swing
her made-up song

Dave Russo
Cary, North Carolina

wife still sleeping
back three flights of stairs
to check the toilet seat

Dee Evetts
New York, New York

with each cast
the fisherman's pants
ride a little lower

Doris Kasson
Belleair Bluffs, Florida

dry season—
    deep scarlet bougainvillea
        piercing the morning glare

Eileen Blas Schaefer
Dededo, Guam

a silent falling
of leaves
        —fever again

Ellen Compton
Washington, D.C.

the first cuckoo:
two long shadows picking
in mother's garden

Emiko Miyashita
Miyamae-ku, Kawasaki, Japan

footprints on sand
the shape
of forgotten happiness

Fay Aoyagi
San Francisco, California

snowy afternoon
two-year-old at the mirror
perfecting his scowl

Francine Porad
Mercer Island, Washington

dead raccoon—
from deep within its eyes
my headlights

Fred Donovan
Stafford, Virginia

The weeds
I meant to pull
in full bloom

Garry Gay
Windsor, California

listening to the rain
the wet spot on the ceiling
begins to drip

Gary Warner
Birmingham, Alabama

in a dream
I wrote a haiku full of wabi—
that's all I recall

George Swede
Toronto, Ontario

freezing rain
field mice rattle the dishes
buson's koto

Gerald Vizenor
Oakland, California

First day at the beach
   seeing again
how white flesh can be.

Graham F. Hollis
Kalamazoo, Michigan

牛部屋に蚊の声暗き残暑かな

ushibeya ni ka no koe kuraki zansho kana

Bashō

in a cowshed
mosquitoes buzzing darkly—
   lingering summer heat

Haruo Shirane, translator
New York, New York

the unpruned orchard
whose apples brush the grass—
a singing sunset

Harvey Hess
Waterloo, Iowa

estate sale
taking the old clock
to a new home

Howard Lee Kilby
Hot Springs, Arkansas

The stillness now
Is gone
Where the heron stood.

Jack Cain
Toronto, Ontario

frozen fingers
draw out a dip stick—
the long night

Jeanne Emrich
Bloomington, Minnesota

autumn moon
one yellow leaf
free of it

Jeffrey Winke
Milwaukee, Wisconsin

paint-peeled shutters
    the drip of a sweater
hung in the sun

Jeff Witkin
Rockville, Maryland

deliberately
I fold up my umbrella
in the spring rain

Jerry Ball
Seal Beach, California

receiving change—
the bill folds in half
on its own

Jim Kacian
Winchester, Virginia

Deer dung on the hill—
A tidy pile reminds us
To tiptoe with care.

Joan Fisher
Evanston, Illinois

war memorial:
the eternal flame's
flickering shadow

Jocelyn A. Conway
Concord, California

chilled fields
four windows blazing
in sunset

John P. Klein
Hometown, Illinois

midsummer
　　stream's grown
　　　　a tunnel

John Martone
Charleston, Illinois

nursing home survey:
for two out of five
it is spring

John Stevenson
Nassau, New York

beneath melting snow
　　　trailing juniper . . .
　　　　　and a red scarf

Joseph Kirschner
Evanston, Illinois

Hardly a ripple
water grey-blue
sky blue-gray

Josip Pasic
Chicago, Illinois

wren's song—
rain on the copper
wind chime

Judson Evans
Holbrook, Massachusetts

let loose
on a commuter train
dandelion seeds

Kris Kondō
Atsugi-shi, Kanagawa, Japan

shorter days—
autumn comes to the
leaves of the bonsai

Kristen Deming
Bethesda, Maryland

full moon descending
into waikiki sand
easter sunrise

Larry Lavenz
Waterloo, Iowa

drought
the sound of surf
    up windless hills

Laurie W. Stoelting
Mill Valley, California

rumble of thunder—
boy still searching for the ball
in the tall grass

Lee Gurga
Lincoln, Illinois

deep crack
of thunder in the rain—
my mother's silence

Lenard D. Moore
Raleigh, North Carolina

pointed church tower
plunged into dark cloud—
first thunder

Lidia Rozmus
Vernon Hills, Illinois

枯朶に烏のとまりけり秋の暮
kareeda ni karasu no tomarikeri aki no kure

Bashō

On a dead limb
squats a crow—
autumn night.

Lucien Stryk, translator
DeKalb, Illinois

the smell of diesel
a fishing boat
appears in the fog

Marc Thompson
Lancaster, Pennsylvania

class reunion
her new hearing aid
clarifies the gossip

Mary Fran Meer
Bellevue, Washington

mid winter
painting my nails the color
of the amaryllis

Margaret Chula
Portland, Oregon

crush on my piano teacher:
dreaming of his long fingers
I bang the white keys

Mauree Pendergrast
Morristown, New Jersey

street sign
on Greenleaf Ave.
turning red

Michael Nickels-Wisdom
Spring Grove, Illinois

summer solstice—
a rack full of hats
at the barbershop

Michael Dylan Welch
Foster City, California

through binoculars
the woman looking at me
through binoculars

Mykel Board
New York, New York

Wild iris
unsheathing themselves
all at once

Nicholaes P. Roosevelt
Storrs, Connecticut

one in the sunlight
              one in the shade
     daisies on my lawn

Nick Avis
Corner Brook, Newfoundland

snowfall
the wings of pigeons fold
into the tree

Pamela Miller Ness
New York, New York

tangled around
the no trespassing sign
poison ivy

Pardee Gunter
Leesburg, Indiana

summer haze—
the faces of the guests
begin to appear

Patricia Donegan
Nakano-ku, Tokyo, Japan

automatic doors:
the blizzard expands
into the lobby

Paul Jung
Mahtomedi, Minnesota

the artist's slow hand
putting another small vein
in the lotus leaf

Paul O. Williams
Belmont, California

cherry blossom time—
a festival booth displays
antique swords

Paul Watsky
San Francisco, California

new grass
two white horses
touching necks

Paul W. MacNeil
Ocala, Florida

TV off
the screen reflects
a living room

Penny Harter
Santa Fe, New Mexico

Memorial day
the music box ballerina   stops
mid-melody

Raffael de Gruttola
Natick, Massachusetts

feeling for a key
in a full pocket—a bit
of blue between clouds

Randal Johnson
Olympia, Washington

campus bench
in the pine tree's shade . . .
an opened letter

Randy M. Brooks
Decatur, Illinois

bright April morning—
the bare jacaranda limbs
hint of blossoming

Rengé / David Priebe
Los Angeles, California

ripples on the stream
carrying the fading light
into a drainpipe

Rick Tarquinio
Nashville, Tennessee

March winds and blue sky
old man with an umbrella
too busy for spring

R. Michael Beatty
South Bend, Indiana

So near . . .
speaking softly
to the passing crane

Robert F. Mainone
Delton, Michigan

first bluebonnets—
old couple on the roadside
picking up cans

Robert Gilliland
Austin, Texas

Gardener by the wall.
He peels a pear for breakfast
sheltered from spring winds

Robert Major
Poulsbo, Washington

nearly dusk
   mist distilling
into drops
   on tips of pines

Robert Spiess
Madison, Wisconsin

searching for my key:
a mosquito inserts
the thinnest pain

Ruth Yarrow
Seattle, Washington

willow baskets
for sale
the scent of rain

Sandra Fuhringer
Hamilton, Ontario

noonday sun
as if the first quart wasn't enough
ripe strawberries

Sara Brant
Ann Arbor, Michigan

winter solstice—
the cat jumps at the sunlight
playing off my watch

S. R. Spanyer
Louisville, Kentucky

all his life the sage
ponders the flowing river—
children jump in

Stan Grotegut
Boulder, Colerado

Autumn leaves
come rushing in . . .
with my party guests.

Susumu Takiguchi
Oxford, England

blossom scent . . .
cannot stop the moon
falling down

Tadashi Kondō
Dorchester, Massachusetts

a junco works
the grass-seed stalk . . .
falling snow

William J. Higginson
Santa Fe, New Mexico

drifting clouds—
on the edge
of the kimono

Yoshie Ishibashi
Nakano-ku, Tokyo, Japan

winter solstice—
the slow curving of your breast
into dawn

Yu Chang
Schenectady, New York

Not So Obvious

by Joseph Kirschner

autumn moon
one yellow leaf
free of it

The author of this poem is Jeffrey Winke, of Milwaukee, Wisconsin. In only a few words Jeffrey's haiku leaves readers with two powerful feelings: freedom and loss. The impact is potent. The moonlight illuminates an ending, reflected in the fallen yellow leaf. The two season words of "autumn moon" and "yellow leaf" may seem redundant to some haiku purists, but the yellow leaf offers a specific marker of the general setting framed by the autumn moon. This pairing of the specific and the more universal lends this haiku depth. We feel a momentary sense of mystery because the antecedent of the word "it" is ambiguous. Whatever "it" may be, the word draws readers to ponder: free of what?

Even the rhythm of the verse contributes to its meaning. The open-mouthed first syllable of "autumn" is closed off by its second syllable, which implies a flow and then an ending. The drawn-out vowel sounds of the first line suggest the season's smooth flow, reinforced by the rhythm of "one yellow leaf," as if to underscore the point. Yet along with seasonal flow comes the season's end, which is rendered pointedly by both the meaning and break in flow of the third line: "free of it."

The indefinite reference of the pronoun "it" may be momentarily uncertain, but the ambiguity offers a depth of meaning in its very indefiniteness. We may assume that "it" refers to the tree from which the leaf had drawn its sustenance. But more seems to be implied. Is the leaf freed from being revealed in the moonlight? Perhaps that leaf distracts us from viewing the moon. Is the verse about the briefness of life, no matter what glow may appear at its end? At least the leaf exhibits a brief colorful glory before the final separation from its source of life. Perhaps the fallen yellow leaf points toward some mystery lying beyond that brief glory at the conclusion of its life. It's as if the leaf is asking if there more to the destiny of living things beyond decay and rot.

As used in this poem, the double season words of "autumn moon" and "yellow leaf" seems to be emphasized as deliberate because of the pronoun's uncertain referent. Not only is the seasonal motif sharpened, but the poem creates a sense of wonder by the questioning that "it" raises.

Suddenly everything is not so obvious. The point of the haiku seems not to have much to do with either seasonal image, or even both. The poem is a finger pointing toward some larger mystery lying beyond the obvious: the sustaining life that the implied tree provides. Thus, despite using common fall imagery, the haiku manages to raise profound questions.

Paperclips

2001

Michael Dylan Welch, Carol Purington, and Larry Kimmel, editors
Karen Klein, ink brush drawings

June 28–July 1, 2001, 90 anthology contributors, one poem each

Conference Location:
Boston Conservatory, Boston, Massachusetts

"A sheaf of haiku may be held together by a paperclip until the clip grows rusty and stains the paper. But age stains do not accumulate on words containing the images and energy of a well-lived moment, nor does age touch the poet who can consistently find words to illuminate the unseen or the overlooked." —*from the introduction*

spring sun—
the carriage horse shakes off
a cloud of dust

A. C. Missias
Philadelphia, Pennsylvania

far down the railroad tracks
the brakeman's lantern
gets lost among the fireflies

Alan Pizzarelli
Garfield, New Jersey

under and over
the creaking pier
a pair of swallows

Angelee Deodhar
Chandigarh, India

rainbow slipping away
a soft breeze
falls on my just-shaved chin

Arizona Zipper
Fryeburg, Maine

spring twilight
the quiet firehouse
at dinner time

Bruce Kennedy
Brooklyn, New York

country farmhouse
an old lawn chair left beside
the family garden

Bruce Ross
Red Deer, Alberta

sushi dinner—
        discussing his sex change
my chopsticks cross

Brynne McAdoo
Morristown, New Jersey

mall about to close—
from each store the clatter
of clerks counting coins

Carlos Colón
Shreveport, Louisiana

opening the fridge
 just a crack
   the cat crowds in

Carl Patrick
New York, New York

taping paper ants
on the linoleum floor
April Fool's Day

Carmen Sterba
Kanagawa-ken, Japan

Good Friday service
A branch of pussywillows
throws spiky shadows

Carol Purington
Colrain, Massachusetts

mammogram waiting room
she rips a page
from a magazine

Carolyn Hall
San Francisco, California

Notre Dame:
twisted postures of tourists
gawking at gargoyles

Charles Trumbull
Evanston, Illinois

a field of snow
crisscrossed with animal tracks
winter reading

Cheryl Burghdurf
Montpelier, Vermont

autumn equinox—
child of my child racing past
without training wheels

Claire Gallagher
Sunnyvale, California

on new snow
long sensuous shadows
of common weeds

Claudia Graf
Clarendon, Ontario

the rusted paperclip
has stained my old poem
wind in the eaves

Cor van den Heuvel
New York, New York

schoolboy's face
at the pawnshop window—
pistols diamonds guitars

Dave Russo
Cary, North Carolina

July 3
street person still wears
a quilted vest

Diane Mayr
Salem, New Hampshire

in the next room
the radio whispers
to no one

Dorothy Howard
Aylmer, Québec

near the porch light
a gecko stops chirping,
a moth disappears

Eileen Blas Schaefer
Dededo, Guam

flower market
the faint click-click
of abacus beads

Ellen Compton
Washington, D.C.

plum rain ends—
on both sidewalks of a street
    the baby carriages

Emiko Miyashita
Kawasaki, Japan

a new summer hat
she may be out
of love

Fay Aoyagi
San Francisco, California

breakfast alone . . .
the dove's feather
he left for me

Ferris Gilli
Orlando, Florida

cold harbor dawn—
a fishmonger slaps a salmon
on the packed ice

Fred Donovan
Rockville, Maryland

the puddles they run thru—
the part of the sky
that shakes

Gary Hotham
Laurel, Maryland

one stone standing
earth trembles . . .
then there were none

George Emlen Roosevelt
Saylorsbury, Pennsylvania

Key West sunset;
unhappy crowd
boos the clouds.

George Pope
Mt. Pleasant, South Carolina

her dung in the snow—
scraping dog arabesques
on macadam

Grace Lazell Hull
Chambersburg, Pennsylvania

古池の蛙老いゆく落葉かな
furuike no kawazu oiyuku ochiba kana

Buson

the frog of the ancient pond
grows old—
    fallen leaves

Haruo Shirane, translator
New York, New York

heat wave breaks
    dark fumbling
for the kicked-off quilt

Hayat Abuza
Northampton, Massachusetts

セザンヌに
　　色盗まれて
　　　　白紫陽花

Sezannu iro nusumarete shiro ajisai

Himeyo Kamiyama
Koyama, Tochigi, Japan

Its color stolen
　　　　by Cézanne
　　　　　　white hydrangea

Hiroaki Sato, translator
New York, New York

egg rolls and hot tea
an Auschwitz survivor
talks of UFOs

Howard Lee Kilby
Hot Springs, Arkansas

166

peeling paint
she sorts the letters
from her youth

Ion Codrescu
Constanta, Romania

argument—
the curling lid
of the empty sardine can

Janeth Ewald
St. Helena, California

quiet afternoon—
working the burrs
from the cow's belly

J. Chris Baltzley
Safety Harbor, Florida

first snow—
the Hawaiian visitor
sticks out her tongue

Jeanne Emrich
Bloomington, Minnesota

telephoto lens
from eye   to eye
  a star

Jeanne Martin
Newton, Massachusetts

first warm day—
two old women bring daisies
to a gravesite

Jim Kacian
Winchester, Virginia

bright winter day
junkyard workers crowd around
an oil drum fire

John Bergstrom
Boston, Massachusetts

glass-topped conference table
  looking up
    their noses

John Stevenson
Nassau, New York

July swelter
in a paint store
rumba of the mixers

Judson Evans
Holbrook, Massachusetts

evening shower
a lightly clothed woman
holding her breasts

Kaji Aso
Boston, Massachusetts

heat lightning
the dampness
along her hairline

Karen Klein
Cambridge, Massachusetts

commuter train
behind the newspaper fold
giggling twins

Kathleen P. Decker
Redmond, Washington

still morning—
a line of snow darkens
every branch

kirsty karkow
Waldoboro, Maine

away from the party din
Jupiter's bold shine
among black boughs

Larry Kimmel
Colrain, Massachusetts

deserted siding
snowflakes flutter
among the empty boxcars

Larry Rungren
Andover, Massachusetts

wild cherry blossoms
the ritual adjustment
of her short skirt

Lee Gurga
Lincoln, Illinois

first summer rain—
a lab full of students
typing their papers

Lenard D. Moore
Raleigh, North Carolina

cemetery on the hill
ten, maybe twenty graves
          with a great view

Lidia Rozmus
Vernon Hills, Illinois

naturalist's talk—
his turkey strut ripples
through the crowd

Linda Jeannette Ward
Coinjock, North Carolina

lunar eclipse
after four years
just meeting the neighbors

Linda Robeck
Amesbury, Massachusetts

sticky afternoon
the old stump
covered with mushrooms

Lori Laliberte-Carey
Tucker, Georgia

outdoor sitting
a yellow jacket vibrates
my meditation bowl

Margaret Chula
Portland, Oregon

Sprinkler-bush spin-off
Water droplets in the breeze
Form an oval patch

Marlene Wenger Roadruck
Greenwood, Indiana

sidewalk sale—
a corner bent over
in the used paperback

Michael Dylan Welch
Foster City, California

January wind
the red ears of the boy
with the black yarmulke

Michael Ketchek
Rochester, New York

gap-toothed
and lying on the sidewalk,
a pocket comb

Michael Nickels-Wisdom
Spring Grove, Illinois

in a shady wood
  the sun touches
  just touches
    a branch

miriam chaikin
New York, New York

the movie ignored
looking for our shadow
on the clouds below

Mykel Board
New York, New York

ash puff—
two brothers
divvy up the third

Nicholaes P. Roosevelt
Storrs, Connecticut

playing checkers . . .
a black butterfly
kings my opponent

Pamela A. Babusci
Rochester, New York

after the snow
scooping a handful
of damp cherry blossoms

Pamela Miller Ness
New York, New York

the NASDAQ plunges—
a dark shadow
between her breasts

Paul David Mena
Cochituate, Massachusetts

midday heat
the ponderous gait
of a stag beetle

Paul MacNeil
Ocala, Florida

175

medieval cliff town—
its most treacherous path stones
well polished

Paul Watsky
San Francisco, California

narrow path
a streak of pollen
on one sleeve

Peggy Willis Lyles
Tucker, Georgia

summer dusk—
how bright the asparagus
on my dinner plate

Penny Harter
Santa Fe, New Mexico

Little pools and brooks
of melting snow in the woods
beside the train tracks.

Peter Foulkes
Worcester, Massachusetts

that path again
snow over
last night's footprints

Raffael de Gruttola
Natick, Massachusetts

a burst of sunlight
beams down on mountain meadow
—grazing horse looks up

Rengé / David Priebe
Los Angeles, California

not intending
to accompany the juggler
accordionist

Richard St. Clair
Somerville, Massachusetts

Meditating:
red koi under the footbridge
dart, then disappear

Rich Schnell
Port Douglas, New York

pool draining—
in the deep end
one last sliver of sun

Rich Youmans
North Falmouth, Massachusetts

Autumn butterfly
our three-second love affair
the red light changes

R. Michael Beatty
South Bend, Indiana

quiet rain
. . . the deeper quiet
of uncut roses

Roberta Beary
Bethesda, Maryland

winter dusk
coyote running   belly low
and silent

Robert Gibson
Centralia, Washington

rope
swing
straight
up
and
down
summer
rain

Robert Zukowski
Panama City, Florida

spring sunshine—
its smell before you see it
old wooden fence

Sarah A. Jensen
Ludington, Michigan

the rice-planting girl
raises her head
like the heron

Shokan T. Kondō
Nakano, Japan

the cranes are flying—
at the neighbouring window
an old man

Sonia Cristina Coman
Constanta, Romania

end of autumn—
finding myself
in a field of thistle

Stanford M. Forrester
Wethersfield, Connecticut

mother's day . . .
the turn
into the cemetery

Susan Scholl
Syracuse, New York

the cat's eyes
   so wide . . .
      for a gnat

Tom Clausen
Ithaca, New York

her sixth month
in the garden she selects
buds over blooms

Wanda D. Cook
Hadley, Massachusetts

fire in the treetops
the truck races down the street
trailing its hoses

William J. Higginson
Santa Fe, New Mexico

old passport
the tug
of my father's smile

Yu Chang
Schenectady, New York

between trains
snowflakes cluster
on the shiny rail

Zeke Vayman
Allston, Massachusetts

Remembering in Silence

by Raffael de Gruttola

breakfast alone . . .
the dove's feather
he left me

As the sun rises in one's life one can relive many experiences that make one's moments of love and caring the journey of a lifetime of faith. This is a faith that couples gain from love—the memories of passion and the instant of passing. Ferris Gilli's moment of truth in remembering her beliefs makes the symbol of a dove's feather poignant. In just a few words her haiku captures the same feeling as the ending of a famous Issa haiku, and we understand that each personal journey is every person's journey . . . and yet!

What makes this thought appealing is the pause in the poet's moment of reflection. This pause bridges the memories that two people share and becomes the reality of caring. In these experiences, the he and she in this poem share a lifetime together or in memory apart.

We often sit alone with our thoughts, searching for the right expression or for a memory of times past. Memories rush back in a poignant "now," bringing with them a simple smile, a chuckle, or even a tear.

Or we can reminisce, especially at breakfast, when the day has yet to begin with its many chores and responsibilities, and muse over our shortcomings or unfulfilled dreams. Here again the dove, a word so close to love, resurfaces.

In the silence of remembering, we stop to reflect and wonder about the simple gesture of the dove's feather left for the poet by an unexplained "he"—a person we can easily imagine to be a spouse or some other relative or friend. But why did this loved one leave such a gift? The symbol changes the meaning of the moment and sustains a feeling of nostalgia and love. Despite being alone at breakfast, perhaps the poet is not really alone after all.

Ferris Gilli, then of Orlando, Florida, has given us many beautiful and heartfelt haiku over the years. This particular poem is a reflection of her gentle ways and manner.

BROCADE OF LEAVES

2003

Michael Dylan Welch and Yu Chang, editors

June 26–29, 2003, 85 anthology contributors, one poem each

Conference Location:
Dalton School, New York, New York

"We know from experience—or at least from a dictionary—that a brocade is a rich silk fabric, often Oriental, with gold and silver patterns. In this book, we are presented with a vibrant brocade of voices, haiku and senryu serving as the gold and silver. These poems spring not just from the Orient, where haiku began, but from poetry weavers from across the United States and Canada, as well as other countries. And this brocade . . . is not just a brocade of silk, but a brocade of leaves, reminding us that nature is central to haiku and related genres of poetry." —*from the introduction*

first forsythia—
workmen chat
from roof to roof

A. C. Missias
Philadelphia, Pennsylvania

off season—
the first snow falls
on empty streets

Adelaide B. Shaw
Scarsdale, New York

left out
in the hailstorm
a pogo stick

Alan Pizzarelli
Bloomfield, New Jersey

cherry blossoms—
a foot bridge spans a stream
    and the milky way

Allen M. Terdiman
Mamaroneck, New York

brief rainstorm—
a gulmohur petal rides
a boy's paper boat

Angelee Deodhar
Chandigarh, India

spring pruning:
I stagger the branches
of the corkscrew hazel

Anita Krumins
Toronto, Ontario

Pilgrims pressed in
dark hallways, lit by candles
and one light bulb.

Anne Elizabeth Evans
Allentown, Pennsylvania

still there
on the snow-bent branch
—lingering leaf

Arlene Teck
Rockaway, New York

stepping into
the undertow
wind chimes

Barry Goodmann
Hackensack, New Jersey

circling Ground Zero
a ring of sequoias
but then I wake up

Brenda J. Gannam
Brooklyn, New York

late for work . . .
the cat's muddy paw print
on my collar

Brian Tasker
Frome, Somerset, England

heavy snowfall
the Brooklyn Bridge
cancelled

Bruce Kennedy
Brooklyn, New York

balmy summer day
a weathervane's faint shadow
on the shingles

Bruce Ross
Bangor, Maine

two different greys
in a frozen boot track
end of winter

Burnell Lippy
Mt. Tremper, New York

ground fog
a pair of headlines
leaving the cemetery

Carlos Colón
Shreveport, Louisiana

full moon
a shadow under the eaves
of the martin box

Carl Patrick
Brooklyn, New York

leaf's single dewdrop
round, alone in still morning
my reflected face

Carolanne Reynolds
West Vancouver, British Columbia

black snake
in the old chicken house
deep breath

Charles Wilton Guy Jr.
Raleigh, North Carolina

library oaks—
a delta of acorns
spreads from the downspout

Chris Baltzley
Safety Harbor, Florida

mirror
the narcissus
leans into itself

Claudia Coutu
Sharbot Lake, Ontario

another autumn
the tailor shop I wrote about
is gone

Cor van den Heuvel
New York, New York

twilight—
carrying batting helmets
in a burlap bag

Dan McCullough
Arlington, Massachusetts

from one shadow
in the croup tent
a bedtime story

Dave Russo
Cary, North Carolina

Salmon fishermen
in the shadows of the bridge
flycast to the sun

David McMurray
Kagoshima, Japan

moon flowers—
i remember a poem
for mother

Deborah Russell
Lutherville, Maryland

back to school
tiny ants swarm
the wad of gum

DeVar Dahl
Magrath, Alberta

above the park wall
the flags of a parade
going past

Doris Heitmeyer
New York, New York

carnival booth
the auxiliary cop
examines the air rifle

Efren Estevez
East Norwich, New York

cries of killdeer
killdeer   mist lifting
over icemelt

Ellen Compton
Washington, D.C.

The universe—
I blow it in all directions
dandelion puff

Garry Gay
Windsor, California

art museum
a pale moth rests
on the window

Gary Warner
Birmingham, Alabama

slack tide—
the click and wheeze
of mussel beds

George Dorsty
Jamesport, New York

After I crack
the third egg into the pan
sunrise

George Swede
Toronto, Ontario

warblers' return
falling apple petals
  reveal the wind

                    Hayat Nancy Abuza
                    Northampton, Massachusetts

river mist
shadows of the geese
I hear

                    Hilary Tann
                    Schuylerville, New York

spring warmth
the moon lights my shadow
on the way home

                    hortensia anderson
                    New York, New York

deep in center field
the earth chills my back
meteor shower

                    James Paulson
                    Narbeth, Pennsylvania

melting snow—
I chat with a stranger
on the bridge

Jeanne Emrich
Bloomington, Minnesota

long winter—
the child's frozen footprint
already outgrown

Jerome Cushman
Victor, New York

apple pie—
what more needs to be said
about my childhood

Jerry Kilbride
Sacramento, California

sleepless night
the burble of a jet
i cannot see

Jim Kacian
Winchester, Virginia

fragrant tea
the stillness of snow
before dawn

Joan Krishnaswami
New York, New York

the day I was away
first bloom
of the day lily

Joette Giorgis
Collegeville, Pennsylvania

the spell check questions them:
    Majdanek, Sobibor,
        Belzec . . .

John Stevenson
Nassau, New York

third trimester
    scanning the cloudy night sky
        for the twins

Judson Evans
Holbrook, Massachusetts

inner city
streetlights outshine
the Leonids

Karen Klein
Cambridge, Massachusetts

outside her door
a scatter of petals
from the stolen blossoms

Karen Sohne
Toronto, Ontario

late-april snow
the branches lift
by sunset

Kathleen Rudawsky
Safety Harbor, Florida

July heat
ice cream cone and I
     melting

        L. A. Davidson
        New York, New York

in this summer heat
my belly a cool melon
where my wife kissed it

        Larry Bole
        Woodside, New York

black caterpillars
crawl up the lambsquarter
forecast of heavy snow

        Larry Lavenz
        Waterloo, Iowa

spiderwort in bloom
"I love you" note
in the wrong envelope

        Lee Gurga
        Lincoln, Illinois

long trip back
from his daughter's dorm—
red winter sunset

Lenard D. Moore
Raleigh, North Carolina

maple trees in bloom—
        the cats rearrange themselves
on the window sill

Linda Porter
West Springfield, Massachusetts

slug on his forehead
the compassionate smile
of the stone Buddha

Margaret Chula
Portland, Oregon

slim stems of April violets:
    one day
    they will own this world

Marilyn Hazelton
Allentown, Pennsylvania

late   to watch the deciding game
  the full moon

Marshall Hryciuk
Toronto, Ontario

after arguing all day
we agree
the moon is full

Mauree Pendergrast
Morristown, New Jersey

spring thaw—
the old scarecrow
a little taller

Michael Dylan Welch
Sammamish, Washington

May Day
by the children's graveyard
call of the cuckoo

Nicholaes P. Roosevelt
Storrs, Connecticut

brocade of leaves . . .
a monk sweeps a path
for the guests

Pamela A. Babusci
Rochester, New York

the wee hours
a quartered apple
browns

Pamela Miller Ness
New York, New York

all-night supermarket
I get the shopping cart
with the shaky front wheel

Paul David Mena
Wayland, Massachusetts

my seated shadow
a butterfly pauses
on the hat

Paul MacNeil
Ocala, Florida

old punk song . . .
I pump my fist
in the gardening glove

Paul Pfleuger Jr.
Brooklyn, New York

summer afternoon
soft thump on the window
ghost of a sparrow

Peggy Heinrich
Bridgeport, Connecticut

scattered stars—
the mist between us
tastes of pine

Peggy Willis Lyles
Tucker, Georgia

another birthday—
I push the candles in
deeper

Penny Harter
Summit, New Jersey

distant snow plow . . .
a chill opening
this morning's news

Randy M. Brooks
Decatur, Illinois

The cliff's dirt edge
       An eroded
sense of self

Regina Weinreich
New York, New York

winter rain sunday
my teenager puts on
fresh pajamas

Roberta Beary
Bethesda, Maryland

The green door, open.
How is it I've never been
caught leaping through it?

Ruth Sabath Rosenthal
New York, New York

Staccato footsteps
Walking off my anger.

Sandy Warren
Ocean City, New York

first warm day
the razor-thin cat scratch
on my wrist

Scott Mason
Chappaqua, New York

old jazz record—
a scratch
    improvises

Stanford M. Forrester
Wethersfield, Connecticut

moving the woodpile—
face to face
with the recluse

S. T. Boyle
Jamesport, New York

all the blossoms
    fallen from the sprig
        I broke for you

Sylvia Forges-Ryan
North Haven, Connecticut

a dove in the sun
picking her feathers
after love-making

tei matsushita scott
Reston, Virginia

buttoning
and unbuttoning her blouse
spring rain

Terry Ann Carter
Ottawa, Ontario

chrysalis
   the old-timer's
   rapt attention

Tom Painting
Rochester, New York

Family Court
a grandmother knits
delicate stitches

Tony Pupello
New York, New York

sunlight
in that one place where
the two branches meet

Wanda D. Cook
Hadley, Massachusetts

hospice
footprints of spring mud
quickly mopped

William Cullen Jr.
Brooklyn, New York

spring rain
rereading my own book
I fall asleep

William J. Higginson
Summit, New Jersey

confluence
a marsh reed sways
with a blackbird

Yu Chang
Schenectady, New York

AROMAS

by Tom Painting

"You must know that there is nothing higher and stronger and more wholesome and good for life in the future than some good memory, especially a memory of childhood, of home. People talk to you a great deal about your education, but some good, sacred memory, preserved from childhood, is perhaps the best education. If a man carries many such memories with him into life, he is safe to the end of his days, and if one has only one good memory left in one's heart, even that may sometime be the means of saving us."
—Fyodor Dostoyevsky, *The Brothers Karamazov*

> apple pie
> what more needs to be said
> about my childhood

This poem is by Jerry Kilbride, who used to live in Sacramento, California. The act of transposing an observation, thought, or feeling into words takes time. All haiku ever written are based on memory whether the poet reaches back a moment or years. Haiku are reflective and, if well crafted, carry meaning to the reader in the present tense. If one arrives at instant understanding when reading a haiku, it is one sure sign that the haiku is a success. Such is the case in this one that reflects on the joy of the poet's formative years.

Beyond the aroma of apple pie, straight from the oven, one can assume Kilbride associates a place and person with this memory that has so defined his early life. Left a mystery, the haiku makes room for the reader to speculate, then begs the question, how would you or I define our childhood in one treasured memory?

fishing with my father
what more needs to be said
about my childhood

Jerry Kilbride's haiku encourages us to look to our youthful years for memories that capture the joy of living. Such recollections have the power to sustain us during the trying times that may come later. We are reminded that life's pleasures are best not forgotten.

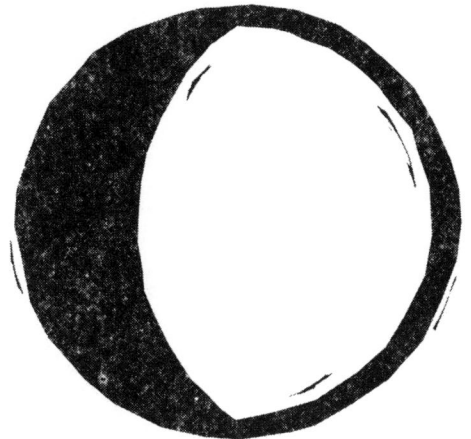

TRACING THE FERN

2005

Michael Dylan Welch and Billie Wilson, editors

September 21–25, 2005, 61 anthology contributors, two poems each

Conference Location:
Fort Worden Conference Center, Port Townsend, Washington

"This book's title reminds us that the carefully chosen words of a memorable haiku are often like tracings of nature—so real that the reader is compelled to participate in the experience that inspired or informed the poem. In each of the haiku and senryu that follow, we hope you enjoy the participation." —*from the introduction*

neige qui fond
sous le soleil d'hiver
le bambou s'érige

snow melting
in the winter sun
—bamboo springs back

douce nuit d'étè
les sanglots de ma fille
le son des trains qui passent

gentle summer night
my daughter's sobs and the sound
of trains passing

Abigail Friedman
Québec City, Québec

tourists moving on—
the store window cat
closes his eyes

the size of
my neighbor's tomatoes
        evening heat

A. C. Missias
Philadelphia, Pennsylvania

golf course at night
deer playing through
the rough

heat wave
even the peacock
is too hot to strut

Angela Terry
Lake Forest Park, Washington

As he tells
of his catch, the fish
unblinking

Garbage dump
the susurrus
of a *TV Guide*

Anita Krumins
Toronto, Ontario

outdoor Shakespeare
above the actors' voices
the call of geese

vacation cabin
all the doors close
by themselves

Bob Moyer
Winston-Salem, North Carolina

adjusting my life
mile after long mile
of thick mist

dune sunset . . .
a gull drops a clam shell
again and again

Bruce Ross
Hampden, Maine

between verses
of Robert Service
squirt of tobacco juice

hotel fire alarm
just me
in pyjamas

Carlos Colón
Shreveport, Louisiana

our extended family
together for the first time . . .
last night's dream

leap for joy
in the artist's ink strokes
friend's recovery

Carmen Sterba
University Place, Washington

back to school—
dusty whelk shells
on the windowsill

late summer
a hermit crab caught
between homes

Carole MacRury
Point Roberts, Washington

prairie dog holes
in the crumbling bluff
empty crab shells

with soft lips
she plucks the purple thistle
—shetland pony

Carol O'Dell
Port Townsend, Washington

barefoot day
the tang
of a thick-skinned orange

sun glint—
I add the green-backed heron
to my lifetime list

Carolyn Hall
San Francisco, California

golf carts
huddled in the service shed
morning chill

a knock at the door
suddenly cicada song
ceases

Charles Trumbull
Evanston, Illinois

crossing a stream
   the bridge
my shadow makes

the cell phone—
a neighbor pulls up weeds
with one hand

Christopher Herold
Port Townsend, Washington

evening dunes
my fingers find the scent
of sand verbena

tide change . . .
my bare footprints
coming and going

Connie Donleycott
Bremerton, Washington

out in the meadow
  she uses her
    "inside" voice

a fungi colony
    ladders
the old maple's trunk

Connie Hutchison
Kirkland, Washington

morning heat
yellow jackets find
   the shotgunned fox

morphine afternoon
white and yellow roses
   on her pillow

Dave Russo
Cary, North Carolina

night rain—
the Navajo waitress
unlooses her hair

today's report
on Dad's balcony tomato—
my nod into the phone

D. Claire Gallagher
Sunnyvale, California

Nimbly climbing
   on the roof, in the raccoon's hands
      grapes.

Meeting in the overflowing café, love blossoms.

Dean Brink
Lacey, Washington

   the dusk of autumn
   one last leaf anchors
      the spider web

   a well-trod path
   gone are the blackberries
      within reach

Dean Summers
Seattle, Washington

summit
meeting
the wind

alone again . . .
noticing a cobweb
in a hidden corner

Dietmar Tauchner
Puchberg, Austria

bright rain puddle
the sun brings mountains
down to earth again

watching the rat
        watch me—
we both run

Doris Thurston
Port Townsend, Washington

a monkey's leap

the forest canopy
shakes down its rain

autumn dusk—
whispers of persimmon leaves
from the road behind

> *Ellen Compton*
> *Washington, D.C.*

an old war song
from an old gramophone
August moon

starry night—
leftovers wrapped
in aluminum foil

> *Emiko Miyashita*
> *Kawasaki, Japan*

forest romp
children shout from chanterelle
to matsutake

new signatures—
the lime-green cast
replaced by hot pink

Francine Porad
Bellevue, Washington

The time changes
sleeping in
with the cats

Apple orchard—
the fragrance
of an old wine

Garry Gay
Windsor, California

231

Horizon moon
the snowman headless
no longer

Leaves turning
she finds the last
brown hair

George Swede
Toronto, Ontario

winter cold—
a model ship's white sails
against the windowpane

clear night—
truck headlights flicker
through guardrail posts

Harry Bose
Pendleton, Oregon

Shoveling compost—
smoke rises from
the inner heap

Plastic blossom—
the wee hummer feeder
is half empty

Ida Freilinger
Bellevue, Washington

spring morning . . .
a tiny feather escapes
the pillow casing

last days of summer . . .
the fishing pier wobbles
beneath my feet

Jeanne Emrich
Edina, Minnesota

ivy bed
one maple seedling
drips dew

golden-ager
counting crows
on his birthday

Jerome Cushman
Victor, New York

the voices i hear aren't talking to me spring twilight

deep space the red shift of my mind

Jim Kacian
Winchester, Virginia

crime scene—
a door to the past
in a strand of hair

grey day—
flashes of white
from startled juncos

Jim Swift
Port Alberni, British Columbia

sixty years on
ground zero ginkgos
still bloom

rest in peace
brown dragonfly—
summer heat

Johnye E. Strickland
North Little Rock, Arkansas

quiet day
the aimless shifting
of cottonwood fluff

trying to play music
from a page of words . . .
dark passageways

Joseph Kirschner
Evanston, Illinois

the sun rises
over the Yolly Bollys;
we walk into it

my staff and I
out for a stroll at dawn
  —autumn chill

Karma Tenzing Wangchuk
Laytonville, California

Red bridles
on a silver gate,
waiting to dance.

Red barn
from the kitchen window—
cats in the wind.

Kate Crowe
Olympia, Washington

summer's passed—
a shadow of the craft's wings
over the beach

after the storm
the air filled with sweet smell
rice stalks fallen down

Kimiyo Tanaka
Matsuyama, Japan

city windows
cat . . . cat . . . cat . . .
dog . . . cat . . .

Hiroshima Day
the bamboo thicket
lost in fog

Lane Parker
San Francisco, California

condensation
on the window
tracing stars

winter darkness
light reflects from the eyes
of a wild thing

Laurie W. Stoelting
Mill Valley, California

red sky
tobacco leaves falling
from the flatbed

first school day—
the petunias circle
the flagpole

Lenard D. Moore
Raleigh, North Carolina

one filament of web
crosses my pathway—
late summer sunshine

home from market—
yellow tulips
instead of vegetables

Lorena Bruff
Bainbridge Island, Washington

deadheading rhodies
her grasp lower
than last year

   at the red light
   moon viewing
through the sun roof

Margaret Chula
Portland, Oregon

field to fence
in the shape of starlings
autumn light

field of crows
   my puppy pauses
which to chase first

Marian Olson
Santa Fe, New Mexico

green water
the ache of my hands
on your oars

returning geese
my heart skips a beat
        skips a beat

Marlene Egger
Salt Lake City, Utah

heirloom portrait
above the rolltop—
his spectacles inside

this year's cattails
among the withered—
I pet them both

Mary Louise Griffith
Portland, Oregon

afternoon hike—
the pussy willows dwindling
from my handful

there, under the awning,
the man who stole
my parking space

Michael Dylan Welch
Sammamish, Washington

New Year:
I clean the shells
she left behind

moon shadows
through the lemon grove
a citrus wind

Michael L. Evans
Port Orchard, Washington

Hunger Moon
I tug the quilt
off the bed

lecture on aging
I choose a chair
near the door

Pamela Miller Ness
New York, New York

After the phone rings there's a cold spot on my hip where your hand was.

Tailgating driver
          demands my attention—
Delicate sliver of moon.

Paul E. Nelson
Auburn, Washington

migratory ducks
I have never
kept a diary

neither apologizing—
the rock garden
in rain

paul m.
Bristol, Rhode Island

rainy morning—
a traffic cop shakes dry
his pen

Valentine's Day
at Ocean Beach the many names
scratched in sand

Paul Watsky
San Francisco, California

after love
she traces the ferns
in the window's frost

full sunlight
all the wrinkles
come out

Penny Harter
Summit, New Jersey

unable to kill or cure
insomnia demons
—then a bird peeps

weary . . .
I gaze into the sideview mirror
my mother stares back

Priscilla Van Valkenburgh
Eden, Utah

everyone's taken
i cha cha
with myself

hospice-by-the-sea
the slow swell
of the interstate

Roberta Beary
Bethesda, Maryland

Leaving San Rafael:
the smell of eucalyptus
misted with the rain

Vacation ended:
abandoned on the railing . . .
collected stones and shells

Robert Major
Poulsbo, Washington

thick fog:
dry rattle of rock
over the edge

barefoot in dew:
across the alpine lake
the sweep of stars

Ruth Yarrow
Seattle, Washington

fall leaves
flutter
faded prayer flags

"avalanche" area
a slide
of asters

Sally Estes
Dallas, Texas

247

new hair color
everyone notices
my glasses

after I pass
the squirrel statue
moves

Terran Campbell
Seattle, Washington

through lace curtains
the blue-black sky—
a car door slams

the glistening red
of a fallen cherry
its insides out

Vicki McCullough
Vancouver, British Columbia

autumn morning—
the shape of the mountain
in the white cloud

a Bach toccata
keeps the fingers moving—
autumn twilight

William J. Higginson
Summit, New Jersey

To remove
or not to remove . . .
the feeding tube

Moments away
from father's dying breath
. . . forgiveness

William Scott Galasso
Kirkland, Washington

ESCAPING

by Christopher Herold

> spring morning . . .
> a tiny feather escapes
> the pillow casing

Jeanne Emrich, the author of this poem, hales from Edina, Minnesota. The key to this irrepressible haiku is the verb "escapes." The word even appears to be escaping the poem, squeezing out from between the other two lines . . . like a feather out of a pillow casing.

My favorite epiphanies are those produced by everyday activities. The commonplace is the wellspring of the finest haiku and it is there we can most abundantly increase our appreciation of life.

Most of you reading this poem will have made many a bed in your time and, unless you have lived your entire life in the tropics, at least some of the bedding materials you've straightened and fluffed up have been down comforters and pillows. Small as the feathers are, their quills are sturdy enough to find weak points in the linens that encase them—a wee hole, or the narrowest opening between stitches in a seam.

There must be tens of thousands of feathers in a given pillow. It is inevitable that now and then the process of bed-making will result in the release of one or two of them. It's as if those few were lucky—the improbable winners of a little lottery. Escaping confinement, the feathers float free, if only for a few moments.

On the surface, this haiku sketches an ordinary material occurrence, yet the poet connected to it at a deeper level. A different sort of liberation was in progress, an emotional one. It's a *spring* morning.

The feather that inspired this poem, tiny as it is, evokes the image of a baby bird—a chick. And aren't all newborn creatures most commonly equated with spring? A down pillow, on the other hand, could be something we use in winter. Following this line of thought, I see the feather's escape from the pillow as spring emerging from winter. So this poem directs us to a more precise time in the cycle of seasons: the transition from winter to spring, with all its attendant hope and joy.

Another notion comes to me. A pillow is a place to rest our heads while we sleep. Those feathers support us while fragmented memories and predispositions to the future roam freely through our gray matter. Imagine that the pillow's contents have become suffused with dreams and nightmares. From what did that feather escape? Into what was it freed?

Your experience of this poem may differ from mine, but I hope you enjoy it every bit as much as I have.

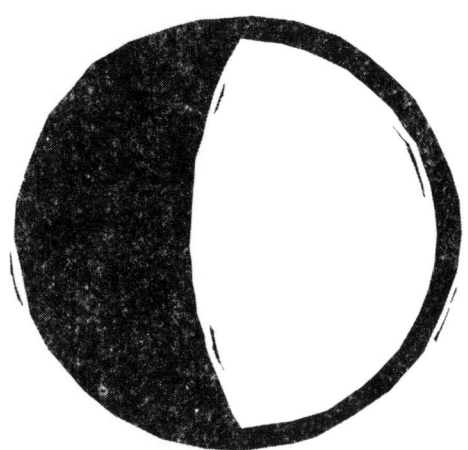

Dandelion Wind

2007

Michael Dylan Welch and Lenard D. Moore, editors
Kate MacQueen, illustrations

August 15–19, 2007, 70 anthology contributors, one poem each

Conference Location:
Hawthorne Inn and Conference Center,
Winston-Salem, North Carolina

"This book's title comes from Garry Gay's poem, and it is to Garry that we dedicate the 2007 Haiku North America conference anthology. It was his idea back in 1990 to start the conference, with the first one taking place in California in the summer of 1991. It immediately became the major gathering of haiku tribes in North America, and has been held around the continent every two years since then. . . . The wish in this book's title poem drifts away like a dandelion seed, as fleeting and ephemeral as the moment that haiku reveres. Unlike that wish, the wish that Garry had for Haiku North America has not drifted away. Instead, it has seeded and taken root. The anthology you hold in your hand, the ninth in the series, is evidence of the continued growth and vibrancy of the haiku community in North America."
—*from the introduction*

morning chill—
crows' feet clatter
on the tin gutter

A. C. Missias
Philadelphia, Pennsylvania

a raven flies off
spruce needles scatter
into a drift of snow

Alan Pizzarelli
Garfield, New Jersey

First day of fishing—
his wife catches
the larger trout.

Alexis Rotella
Arnold, Maryland

teakettle whistle
on the way to the stove
she touches his knee

Bob Moyer
Winston-Salem, North Carolina

Colonial gravestone
all that's left on the front
weathered lines

Bruce Ross
Hampden, Maine

Central Park
a juggler upside down
in my watch crystal

Carl Patrick
Brooklyn, New York

deepening autumn
the strawman's smile
tightens

Carlos Colón
Shreveport, Louisiana

impending surgery—
this unexpected bloom
of autumn poppies

Carolyn Hall
San Francisco, California

suddenly now
an abundance of squirrels
thin shadows of trees

Charles Trumbull
Evanston, Illinois

sequoia
we stand inside
counting rings

Charlie Smith
Raleigh, North Carolina

extra innings
the setting sun lights the underside
of a high fly ball

Cor van den Heuvel
New York, New York

spitting for distance—
a watermelon seed
clings to her nose

Curtis Dunlap
Mayodan, North Carolina

camera obscura
   clouds across
      her bare shoulders

Dave Russo
Cary, North Carolina

chewing their gum
in rhythm
old couple

David G. Lanoue
New Orleans, Louisiana

hospital room
taking the kids' get-well drawings
off her wall

Efren Estevez
East Norwich, New York

brake lights
of a country school bus
blackberry blossoms

Ellen Compton
Washington, D.C.

summer stars
a hint of clover
in the bull's breath

Ferris Gilli
Marietta, Georgia

Dandelion wind
another wish
drifts away

Garry Gay
Santa Rosa, California

Freshly mowed
the cemetery grass—
a tombstone's birthday

George Swede
Toronto, Ontario

Saturday morning
AARP calls
interrupting their sex

James Patrick Haynes
Glasgow, Kentucky

first morning coffee
somewhere on a mountainside
bean pickers sing

Janelle Barrera
Key West, Florida

after the rain
dining on its land
the hare

Janick Belleau
Longueuil, Québec

waiting room—
slipping the renewal card
from a magazine

Jim Kacian
Winchester, Virginia

beyond the trail
the sound of the creek
beckons me

Joette Giorgis
Collegeville, Pennsylvania

the pale undersides
of purple sandpipers . . .
waxing moon

John Barlow
Liverpool, England

the hippopotamus under the cumulus

John Levy
Tucson, Arizona

warm breezes
seem responsible
for the way she walks

John Stevenson
Nassau, New York

she refuses
his kiss
neon moon

Johnette Downing
New Orleans, Louisiana

morning wind
a woodpecker's staccato
between gusts

Johnye E. Strickland
North Little Rock, Arkansas

severe drought
only the steady shrushh
of a cottonwood

Joseph Kirschner
Evanston, Illinois

on the rocky beach
another eagle feather
completes the dance fan

Kaakwdagaan (Donna Foulke)
Leesburg, Virginia

outside wind chimes ring
inside skin on skin, a soft
moon pauses, listens

Kalamu ya Salaam
New Orleans, Louisiana

night rain
the way these worries
pool and seep

Kate MacQueen
Chapel Hill, North Carolina

mouse released
from the humane trap
. . . the owl's shadow

Laquita Wood
Washington, D.C.

blackberry picking—
not yet able to say
I love you

Lee Gurga
Lincoln, Illinois

summer evening
coarseness of gingham prints
in the quilt

Lenard D. Moore
Raleigh, North Carolina

calm lake
geese landing
on clouds

Lidia Rozmus
Vernon Hills, Illinois

paper kites—
river otters wound up
in a helix

Linda Galloway
Encino, California

wrought-iron lamppost
tangled in ivy
evening light

L. Teresa Church
Durham, North Carolina

the moon tonight:
even the footprints
glowing

Marilyn Hazelton
Allentown, Pennsylvania

this rainbow day:
the baby in a sling
begins to fret

Matthew Paul
London, England

sunset
    colors sink and rise
        at the koi pond

Michael Rehling
Livonia, Michigan

fading sunset—
still the shine
on high-tension wires

Michael Dylan Welch
Sammamish, Washington

midday
the tortoise halfway
round its pen

Michele Root-Bernstein
East Lansing, Michigan

new girlfriend—
spilled sand from the Gobi
now in the vacuum

Mykel Board
New York, New York

scorpio moon . . .
airing out this month's
heartaches

Pamela A. Babusci
Rochester, New York

morning dew
wildflower names
we learned yesterday

paul m.
Bristol, Rhode Island

country churchyard
folding chairs
on new sod

Paul MacNeil
Ocala, Florida

far desert mountains—
their secrets shrouded
in hazy blue

Paul O. Williams
Hayward, California

tornado watch
she reads her cat the story
of the Lion King

Peggy Willis Lyles
Tucker, Georgia

January thunder—
by the cellar window
the smell of skunk

Penny Harter
Summit, New Jersey

twilight
deepening
the space between the goalposts
painted on a wall

Philip Rowland
Tokyo, Japan

sun through the mist
slap of the oars echoing
against the shore

Raffael de Gruttola
Natick, Massachusetts

someone
    already here
peonies on Mama's grave

Randy M. Brooks
Decatur, Illinois

returning bones
a stone unwinds
in the breeze

Richard Gilbert
Kumamoto, Japan

blackbirds
under a bridge a puddle
nearly dry

Richard Straw
Cary, North Carolina

lovers' initials
splitting another log
for the fire

Robert McNeill
Winchester, Virginia

losing myself
in purple heat
. . . hydrangea blossoms

Roberta Beary
Washington, D.C.

budding bush
the young boy's hair
grows again

Scott Glander
Glenview, Illinois

heat wave . . .
negotiating roots
to the lake

Scott Mason
Chappaqua, New York

we set sail
in tall grass
no air stirs

Sonia Sanchez
Philadelphia, Pennsylvania

sudden downpour . . .
we quarrel
beneath the crabapple

Stanford M. Forrester
Windsor, Connecticut

from an upstairs balcony
arms thrust a potted begonia
into the rain

Susan Broili
Durham, North Carolina

third star rising
above the same tree
Orion's belt

Tami Fraser
Salt Lake City, Utah

windows blurred
with September rain
—another curtain

Tara Betts
Pearl River, New York

stepping out on ice
my mother's cane
first

Terry Ann Carter
Ottawa, Ontario

a white pigeon
alights on a roofridge
and strolls

Thomas Heffernan
Laurinburg, North Carolina

parting hug
a cicada shell
near the maple's root

Wanda D. Cook
Hadley, Massachusetts

after the Leonids
a falling leaf sets
the grassblade quivering

William J. Higginson
Summit, New Jersey

toll booth
she lets go
of my hand

Yu Chang
Schenectady, New York

A FEW MOLECULES

by Dave Russo

> summer stars
> a hint of clover
> in the bull's breath

This poem comes to us from Ferris Gilli, of Marietta, Georgia. The sense of smell is one of the oldest ways of knowing. Even one-celled animals use an ancestral sense of smell to swim in a promising direction. Odors come into our noses and wander the oldest corridors of our brains, spreading the news, stirring memories in forgotten corners.

Some scents bring specific memories. Cotton candy reminds me of Zsa Zsa, my first real girlfriend, who ran a cotton candy stand at a local amusement park. When I smell that sugar in the air, I can almost hear the Lakeside roller coaster rising and falling, almost taste the luscious pink lip gloss of young love.

Some scents go straight to the heart of a new experience. That's how scent operates for me in Ferris's haiku. The first line, "summer stars," is a visual image—a broad expanse of night sky. It's also a seasonal reference that sets the poem "in the big world of season," in H. F. Noyes's phrase—and at the same time, places the poem in the small world of other haiku that have used this traditional reference to summer.

The next lines bring the poem down to earth, to a field where a bull is out to pasture. We are close enough to smell "a hint of clover" in the bull's breath, to breathe in the connection between the bull and the clover he is eating. It's a warm summer night, so it's easy for the connections to multiply between the bull, the clover, us, and the multitude of stars above.

It's surprising what a few molecules wafting to our noses on the night air—and a few words on the page—can do.

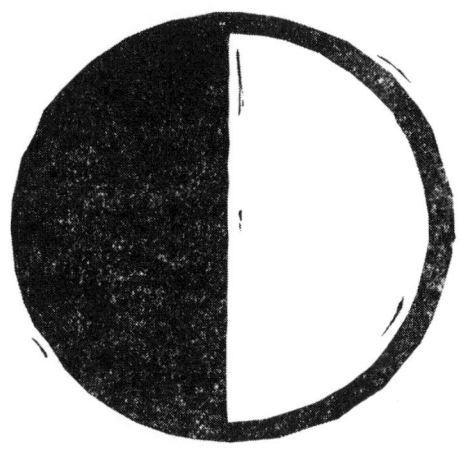

Into Our Words

2009

Michael Dylan Welch and Grant D. Savage, editors
Peter Vernon Quinter, artwork

August 5–9, 2009, 90 anthology contributors, one poem each

Conference Location:
National Library of Canada, Ottawa, Ontario

"No one was ever more in his element at Haiku North America conferences than William J. Higginson. Always the quintessential haiku poet, scholar, enthusiast, advocate, translator, and critic, Bill found such a stimulating and inspiring outlet for his passions and talents at this conference that he surely wished Haiku North America happened multiple times every year instead of just once every two years. He was, too, the only person who had been to all nine conferences since it began in 1991. When he passed away in October of 2008, Bill left a gaping void not just in Haiku North America, but in the entire haiku community worldwide. It is therefore fitting that we dedicate this tenth HNA anthology, *Into Our Words*, to William J. Higginson."
—*from the introduction*

mise en abîme
mes seuls cheveux blancs
dans tous les miroirs

my hair white
reflected infinitely
between the mirrors

André Duhaime
Gatineau, Québec

warm spring night—
alone, digging deep
into the ice cream carton

Angela Leuck
Verdun, Québec

283

farmer's market—
a fruit vendor's child astride
the largest watermelon

Angelee Deodhar
Chandigarh, India

plum cake
the educated voices
of my guests

Anita Krumins
Toronto, Ontario

the roar of traffic
black slug asleep
in Queen Anne's Lace

Betty Warrington-Kearsley
Ottawa, Ontario

Wall Street collapse—
the old couple still
feeding the birds

Bill Pauly
Dubuque, Iowa

a fine rain . . .
the young robins try out
a new-mowed lawn

Bruce Ross
Hampden, Maine

my new
memory
Google

Carlos Colón
Shreveport, Louisiana

first snowman—
a toddler's breath
on the windowpane

Carmen Sterba
University Place, Washington

the mailbox
still expecting a letter
from Mom

Carolyn Coit Dancy
Pittsford, New York

Milky Way
his reluctance
to hold my hand

Carolyn Hall
San Francisco, California

sunflower field
all the windmills
face the same way

Charles Trumbull
Santa Fe, New Mexico

between
pieces of sky
new leaves

Christine Nelson
Athabasca, Alberta

downtown
cherry trees are blooming
no trace of you

Claire Dufresne
Montréal, Québec

in this gentle rain
aquilegia
pinking the garden

Claudia Coutu Radmore
Carleton Place, Ontario

Cree boy
  pushing a tiny skateboard
    along the frozen rail

Dave Russo
Cary, North Carolina

words unspoken—
smoke hovers round the mouth
of the volcano

David Burleigh
Tokyo, Japan

Not a leaf stirring
the old dog
noses a bone

David Elliott
Factoryville, Pennsylvania

long day
the whore on the curb
sits

David G. Lanoue
New Orleans, Louisiana

Summer gone
returning *The Beach*
the top shelf

David McMurray
Kagoshima, Japan

airshow
a flock of pigeons
in formation

Deanna Tiefenthal
Rochester, New York

a velcroed drape
—and whatever else—
separates first class

Deb Koen
Rochester, New York

matilija poppies
the appliance repairman
comes the wrong day

Deborah P Kolodji
Temple City, California

御仏の御鼻の先へつらら哉
mihotoke no mihana no saki e tsurara kana

Issa

Buddha on the moor,
At the tip of his nose
Hangs an icicle.

Dennis Maloney, translator
Lake View, New York

heat wave—
the cow's udder
hangs in the pond

DeVar Dahl
Magrath, Alberta

the bee hesitates
between the Hawaiian shirt
and rhododendrons

Diane Descôteaux
Saint-Nicéphore, Québec

the moon
not quite full
but full enough

Dina E. Cox
Markham, Ontario

I can't remember
his Buddhist death name . . .
watering father's garden

Emiko Miyashita
Kawasaki City, Japan

mid-meeting the pressure released from a soda can

Eve Luckring
Los Angeles, California

hillside peas
did I ever wish
to be a man?

Fay Aoyagi
San Francisco, California

    trees growing
out of rock
    I give in to him

Francine Banwarth
Dubuque, Iowa

The merry-go-round
turns a few more times
as they walk away

Garry Gay
Windsor, California

setting sun—
the mountain's shadow creeps
    into our words

Gary Hotham
Scaggsville, Maryland

musical chimes
with each passing breeze
a new song

Gill Foss
Carp, Ontario

a haunting song
from an unseen bird
long obit section

George Swede
Toronto, Ontario

dry pine needles
I walk in the hollow
dug by slaves

Glenn G. Coats
Prospect, Virginia

moonlit pool
from the silence
a waterfall

Grant D. Savage
Ottawa, Ontario

fresh asparagus
up from the urinal
farmer's market

Guy Simser
Kanata, Ontario

a calendar
above your dusty workbench—
your birthday forever

Heather MacDonald
Ottawa, Ontario

among the sandals
the morning after
stilettos

Henry Brann
Audubon, New Jersey

honeymoon site
grandmother revisits
by herself

Huguette Ducharme
Saint-Pie, Québec

moving in
    wondering how all our stuff fits
        together

Ian Marshall
State College, Pennsylvania

Evening gathering
The dead cedar alive
with parenting crows

Inga Uhlehmann
White Rock, British Columbia

slow summer rain . . .
a different trainee
at the discount store

Janelle Barrera
Key West, Florida

lonely in my canoe
adrift on the lake
blue dragonfly

Janick Belleau
Longueuil, Québec

cold March moon
appears . . . disappears
the long drive home

Jerome Cushman
Victor, New York

biodôme
devant la toilette des dames
querelle d'oiseaux

biodome
outside the ladies' washroom
two birds fighting

> Jessica Tremblay
> Burnaby, British Columbia

a crow's caw in the stone circle older than the woods

> Jim Kacian
> Winchester, Virginia

spring break
I work alone
in the coffeehouse

> Joe Kirschner
> Evanston, Illinois

loud peace protest
  drives away
all the mourning doves

Joey Connolly
Las Vegas, Nevada

  those of money
  and those of rags
their sandals in a single pile

John Brandi
El Rito, New Mexico

summer solstice
a note beyond
the singer's range

John Stevenson
Nassau, New York

passing spring
turtle laying eggs
on the traffic island

Judson Evans
Holbrook, Massachusetts

Lily of the valley
bowing in the misty rain
fragrance permeates the air

Kaoru Fujimoto
Tokyo, Japan

no path goes there
wild orchid

Karen Sohne
Toronto, Ontario

seagulls
on the Triple X marquee—
trash day

Kathleen O'Toole
Takoma Park, Maryland

weighing
the peach's cool sweetness
in my palm

kris moon kondō
Kiyokawa, Japan

cemetery sunset—
I'm the only father visiting
this Father's Day

> *Lenard D. Moore*
> *Raleigh, North Carolina*

on paper
the tree hugger's
agenda

> *LeRoy Gorman*
> *Napanee, Ontario*

the boat
at the very end of the wharf—
and two moons

> *Luce Pelletier*
> *Saint-Basile-le-Grand, Québec*

second honeymoon
taking pictures
of each other

> *Marco Fraticelli*
> *Pointe Claire, Québec*

sudden gust
the lean of bamboo
as one leaf detaches

Margaret Chula
Portland, Oregon

in tiny sandals
I walk to school
lilac smell

Margot Gallant
Ottawa, Ontario

my voice begins
further down in my throat
visiting home

Marilyn Hazelton
Allentown, Pennsylvania

shadow of a moth
        past the blinds

oriole song

> Marshall Hryciuk
> Toronto, Ontario

last week's lilacs
under cat shit
in my garbage

> Melanie Noll
> Ottawa, Ontario

Valentine's Day—
a few clicks
of the swan's beaks

> Michael Dylan Welch
> Sammamish, Washington

news of Hubble—
slicing a pear
for its stars

Michele Root-Bernstein
East Lansing, Michigan

pluie chaude d'été
nous ralentissons le pas
vers la maison

hot summer rain
we slow down our walk
home

Micheline Beaudry
Boucherville, Québec

long shadows—
geese leave
ahead of the snow

Mike Montreuil
Gloucester, Ontario

a prism
  in my eyelash
morning snowfall

Michael Rehling
Livonia, Michigan

summer heat . . .
  the sizzle at the end
    of a good cigar

Naia
Oceanside, California

    leaves on the park bench
  an abandoned walking cane
leans up against it

Nick Avis
St. John's, Newfoundland

old family photos
the weeping willow
so much smaller then

Pamela Cooper
Montréal, Québec

before leaving
attaching name tags
to all her dolls

Pat Benedict
Calgary, Alberta

into the darkness
the whisper
of silver grass

Patricia Donegan
Evanston, Illinois

one of the road crew
resting his eyes
spring meadow

paul m.
Bristol, Rhode Island

last light
the wing-whistle
of mourning doves

Paul MacNeil
Ocala, Florida

in the squeaking cold
breath and walk
both shorter

Pearl Pirie
Nepean, Ontario

train whistle—
I remember the warmth
of your hand

Penny Harter
Mays Landing, New Jersey

railway museum
the set of tracks ends
at the fence

Philomene Kocher
Kingston, Ontario

lupine
    and the *Canadian*
crossing the mountain valley

        Rich Schnell
        Port Douglas, New York

at the memorial,
a white teddy bear
in the fog

        Rick Black
        Highland Park, New Jersey

rainy day
the bus driver bounces
in her seat

        Roberta Beary
        Washington, D.C.

stiffly he bends old joints
to pick up a penny
for all he's worth

        Robin Palley
        Philadelphia, Pennsylvania

rising mercury
our jogging circuit
     all uphill

Scott Mason
Chappaqua, New York

after the thunderstorm
double rainbows
and a well-washed picnic

Sheila M Ross
Gatineau, Québec

casting about
for an honest answer—
mother's silence

Susan Antolin
Walnut Creek, California

too cold for planting
even my dog shivers, skirts
the freshly turned grave

Sylvia Adams
Ottawa, Ontario

Canada Day heat wave
the dancer takes off
her earrings

Terry Ann Carter
Ottawa, Ontario

Lorca, Brewster, and Wright: On the Edge of Haiku

by Terry Ann Carter

> no path goes there
> wild orchard

In his brilliant lecture "Play and Theory of the Duende," Frederico Garcia Lorca attempts to shed light on the inexplicable sadness that lives in the heart of certain works of art. "All that has dark sound has duende," he wrote. "That mysterious power that everyone feels but no philosopher can explain." Later he wrote, ". . . where is the duende? Through the empty archway a wind of the spirit enters, blowing insistently on the heads of the dead; in search of new landscapes and unknown accents: a wind with the odour of a child's saliva, crushed grass, and Medusa's veil, announcing the endless baptism of freshly created things."

This poem is by Karen Sohne, of Toronto, Ontario. For me, her haiku, from the 2009 Haiku North America anthology *Into Our Words*, emits duende. There's a dark resonance (wild orchid) with "a wind of the spirit" (no path goes there). Perhaps it is the mystery that lies in the heart of this haiku that pushes it—and me—to the edge.

Canadian poet Elizabeth Brewster is known for her poem "The Silent Scream." It describes a time in her youth when she almost drowned in a quicksand of sawdust. When she opened her mouth, she had no voice. Sohne's poem is a silent scream for me. A push to try to understand the path that doesn't go there. The edge of the woodpile. The slippage.

Brewster wrote that the "shadow of death came into my mind even in infancy." Is "the path that does not go there" an echo of death? It certainly holds a question at its core.

In an interview for *The Paris Review*, Charles Wright, poet laureate of the United States, alludes to a photograph of his wife in Verona, Italy, 1955, on his mantelpiece, alongside a page from an old edition of *Inferno*, Canto XXIV. He explains, "What I look at has everything to do with what I write." I was moved by this quotation and pondered the essence of Sohne's haiku even further. What was she looking at? Was there a wild orchid in her presence? How did she find this edge?

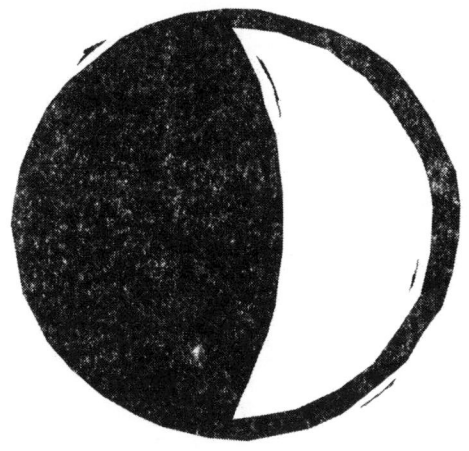

STANDING STILL

2011

Michael Dylan Welch and Ruth Yarrow, editors
Dejah Léger, illustrations

August 3–7, 2011, 74 anthology contributors, one poem each

Conference Location:
Seattle Center, Seattle, Washington

"The 2011 conference theme of 'Fifty Years of Haiku' reminds us that it has been five solid decades that English-language haiku has flourished in North America, with the first haiku journal having started in 1963.This theme also connects us to the location of the 2011 conference at Seattle Center, at the foot of Space Needle, which opened for the World's Fair in 1962. With fifty years of creativity and increasing numbers of poets and poems to celebrate, the Haiku North America conference demonstrates that haiku poets do not stand still in their development and appreciation for this rewarding genre of poetry."
—*from the introduction*

the immigrant woman's
   sorrow so private
  I put down my pen

> *Abigail Friedman*
> *Arlington, Virginia*

ebb tide . . .
the blue heron
wrapped in stillness

> *Angela Terry*
> *Lake Forest Park, Washington*

push mower
cuts through the dandelions
sun-dappled green

> *Ann Spiers*
> *Vashon, Washington*

modern lovers—
she interrupts the kiss
for the cell phone

Astrid Andreescu
Hampden, Maine

shipped oars
we drift with the jellyfish
through her ashes

Billie Dee
San Diego, California

Carpathians
a haystack covered
with blankets

Bruce Ross
Hampden, Maine

barefoot summer . . .
a drop of honeysuckle
on my tongue

> *Cara Holman*
> *Portland, Oregon*

shredding
my former life
retirement

> *Carlos Colón*
> *Shreveport, Louisiana*

two sand dollars
left by this morning's tide—
no more or less

> *Carmen Sterba*
> *University Place, Washington*

empty nest
the fist-curled leaves
of a red maple

> *Carolyn Hall*
> *San Francisco, California*

grass shoots
  deer's breath
  just above them

Ce Rosenow
Eugene, Oregon

worked silver necklace—
I remember the way she looked
fifty years ago

Charles Trumbull
Santa Fe, New Mexico

scribbling pens
to find one that works
winter trees

Cherie Hunter Day
Cupertino, California

to-do list
the cat also content
to sleep on it

Christopher Herold
Port Townsend, Washington

fork in the trail
we trespass into
        cicadas

Connie Hutchison
Kirkland, Washington

the electric fan
turns from the boxscores to
the fashion page and back

Cor van den Heuvel
New York, New York

reflecting pool
I wonder about my life
in that other world

C. R. Manley
Bellevue, Washington

harried Monday
a white butterfly
flits by

Daphne Ashling Purpus
Vashon, Washington

first cup of decaf—
the morning twilight
a bit less purple

David Ash
Mukilteo, Washington

sunset—
the children make the beach
nude

David G. Lanoue
New Orleans, Louisiana

sidewalk ATM
a deposit picked up
by the spring breeze

Deborah P Kolodji
Temple City, California

quiet woods—
he turns to kiss me
through a snowflake

Dejah Léger
Shoreline, Washington

sweet grass and cedar: woven
when the settlers came
her gather basket

Dianne Garcia
Seattle, Washington

spring waterfall . . .
the morning sun splashes
from my hands

Don Baird
Palmdale, California

Brisk west wind,
yet the meadow grass sways
both ways

Don Wentworth
Pittsburgh, Pennsylvania

full moon
scuttling past clouds—
silent swoop of bat

Doris Lynch
Bloomington, Indiana

流木の軽さ白さや南風吹く
ryūboku no karosa shirosa ya minami fuku

the lightness
of the driftwood—
evening southerly

Emiko Miyashita
Kawasaki, Japan

deep ruts
under the children's swing:
end of summer

Ernesto V. Epistola
Sarasota, Florida

downpour
searching the lobby carpet
for a sense of humor

Eve Luckring
Los Angeles, California

distant whistle—
I poke the silence
of a cicada's shell

Fay Aoyagi
San Francisco, California

Spring galaxy—
the windup robot
takes one more step

Garry Gay
Windsor, California

Grandma's face
in the window above the sink
    distant stars

Gene Myers
Rockaway, New Jersey

咲き初めのくちなしの白母に供え
sakizone no kuchinashi no shiro haha ni soe

first gardenia—
I place it on the table
by mom's photo

Hana Fujimoto
Tokyo, Japan

skin-tight bathing suits
for the young
dog days of summer

Janis Lukstein
Rancho Palos Verdes, California

rowing
the stars overhead
the stars below

Jay Friedenberg
New York, New York

twilight—
the crows outlast
the gardener

Jay Gelzer
Seattle, Washington

a cell phone
with an obituary
at the cliff's edge

Jerry Ball
Walnut Creek, California

sieste
une mouche
sur le dos

nap time
a fly
on my back

Jessica Tremblay
Vancouver, British Columbia

the earth mother and always some question who's the father

Jim Kacian
Winchester, Virginia

pine boughs sweeping in snow our last talk

Jim Westenhaver
Tacoma, Washington

violet fireweed
consumes the hillside—
summer heat

Joan D. Stamm
Eastsound, Washington

autumn dusk
fallen leaves have come to rest
in the graveyard

Johnny Baranski
Vancouver, Washington

first fireworks
she turns her face
to mine

Joshua Beach
Sammamish, Washington

fall diagnosis
the dahlia bulbs remain
in the ground

Julie Warther
Dover, Ohio

scattered dominos
new constellations
to disagree about

Katharine Grubb Hawkinson
Seattle, Washington

rope swing
across the river,
across the years

Kathleen Tice
Kent, Washington

full moon
the fox re-sorts
the recycling

kjmunro
Whitehorse, Canada

tonight
shooting star's path
my path

Lidia Rozmus
Vernon Hills, Illinois

a light snowfall—
grandpa waves his hand
on the platform

Makoto Nakanishi
Matsuyama, Japan

beachcombers
the sea takes back
all their discards

Margaret Chula
Portland, Oregon

American goldfinches
yellow bellies
against blue sky

Maria Schuchardt
Tucson, Arizona

city passersby
stare at haiku poets
standing still

Marilyn Hazelton
Allentown, Pennsylvania

morning mist—
wind shifts
the mountain peak

Marilyn Sandall
Seattle, Washington

midsummer's day
this heavy
sweet-bee heat

Marjorie Buettner
Chisago City, Minnesota

the fly's wings

raising
settling

the dust

Melissa Allen
Madison, Wisconsin

botanical garden
and the bee
picks me

Merilyn Peruniak
Athabasca, Alberta

a show of hands
in the jury room . . .
winter light

Michael Dylan Welch
Sammamish, Washington

headstones
almost touched
by April swallows

Mike Dillon
Indianola, Washington

癌検査難なし帰路に買う日記
gan kensa nan nashi kiro ni kau nikki

trouble-free cancer exam
on the way home
I acquire a diary

Minako Noma
Matsuyama, Japan

covered bridge
the plaque says nothing
about a sparrow's nest

paul m.
Bristol, Rhode Island

scarlet leaf
curled in the spider web—
I sleep alone

Penny Harter
Mays Landing, New Jersey

drone of flies
decomposing
my dreams

Raúl Sanchez
Seattle, Washington

drinking radiation no risk of on the news in Japan drinking rain

Richard Gilbert
Kumamoto, Japan

no trespassing . . .
prickly pear blooming on both sides
of barbed wire

Richard Tice
Kent, Washington

sketching wild orchids—
slowly I sense
their sweet smell

Ruth Yarrow
Seattle, Washington

crooked alder
frames the opposite shore—
white refinery smoke

Sheila Sondik
Bellingham, Washington

Mother's Day—
flowers without thorns
in the psych ward

Susan Antolin
Walnut Creek, California

gulls gang the Golden Gate deafening memories

Susan Diridoni
Kensington, California

I tell him
he does too much—
overflowing flower basket

Tanya McDonald
Woodinville, Washington

wood grain of the door
suddenly a forest grove
inside my room

Terran Campbell
Seattle, Washington

a Chopin étude
on late-night radio
pale lilies in a vase

Terry Ann Carter
Ottawa, Ontario

floating mist
the odd sound of
my new address

Tracy Koretsky
Bellevue, Washington

deepening sunset
on the sideboard
last year's canned peaches

Wanda D. Cook
Hadley, Massachusetts

numbers on his arm . . .
a grandchild asks
how he got them

William Scott Galasso
Edmonds, Washington

EMOTIONAL LEAPS

by Angela Terry

scribbling pens
to find one that works
winter trees

The phone rings. You pull out a pen to take a message or perhaps doodle a bit, depending on the caller. The first pen doesn't work, and you test another one. Something you do so unconsciously that it is almost an automatic act, with no thought given to it unless it goes on too long, and then perhaps you start to feel a bit frustrated.

With this haiku by Cherie Hunter Day, of Cupertino, California, I visualize a container sitting next to the phone filled with a variety of pens. You (the person in the poem) randomly pull out one after another to find one that works, and suddenly look out a window. Such an everyday action, and then that "aha!"—that view of winter trees. You stop and realize where you are and what you are seeing. You go off autopilot and into the moment, really noticing the trees themselves in their winter splendor: the solidness of the trunk, the shape of the branches, the texture of the bark. Maybe a few leaves have hung on, maybe there's a small nest left over from last year resting comfortably in a tree's protective branches. Or perhaps you're looking at evergreens with a sprinkling of fresh snow, casting dark shadows on the ground around them.

This haiku grabs the senses. It's filled with the ending *s* sounds of *pens*, *works*, and *trees*, and starts with an *s* as well in *scribbling*. And the *w* sounds of *one*, *works*, and *winter* give the poem a cohesiveness and rhythmic flow. You can feel the smoothness of each pen as it is picked up and then put back down, and at the sight of the winter trees, the day becomes a little lighter, a little brighter.

While the 2011 HNA anthology *Standing Still* contained many exceptional haiku, this one stood out for me because it so perfectly caught that emotional leap from the everyday to the exceptional, a moment that made me stop, stand still, and really see.

CLOSE TO THE WIND

2013

Michael Dylan Welch and William Hart, editors
Naia, illustrations

August 14–18, 2013, 97 anthology contributors, one poem each

Conference Location:
Queen Mary, Long Beach, California

"We hope you enjoy reading the poems in this anthology, our second largest in more than twenty years of biennial HNA conferences. As with all previous anthologies, we've arranged the poems by each poet's first name. Even when gales are lashing and we're sailing close to the wind, here's hoping we can maintain our close-knit spirit of community and always remain on a first-name basis." —*from the introduction*

Bach cello
swallows sky mind
evening splinters

Ambika Talwar
Los Angeles, California

this morning
angel wings
on the rooftop

Andrea Eldridge
Claremont, California

the river fills with stars . . .
we always thought
we would have tomorrow

Angela Terry
Lake Forest Park, Washington

a spider strand
catches the last of the sun
the clamor of mynahs

Angelee Deodhar
Chandigarh, India

our wedding rings
in the velvet box—
forked roads

Anita Curran Guenin
San Diego, California

perfectly pawdicured pet with mismatched socks

Anna Kondō
Atlanta, Georgia

Oklahoma kids
buried alive in rubble
their last day of school

Barbara Hay
Ponca City, Oklahoma

summer dusk—
sunset and moonrise
in one breath

Beki Reese
Costa Mesa, California

Bohemian waxwings—
and I didn't even have
a bucket list

Billie Wilson
Juneau, Alaska

a few petals
left by the sweeper . . .
sunset clouds

Bill Kenney
Whitestone, New York

midnight train
even the transient
keeps up appearances

Brosnan Rhodes
Los Angeles, California

after heart surgery
they finish the mandala
jigsaw puzzle

Bruce H. Feingold
Berkeley, California

Muir Woods . . .
stepping into
his words

Carol Judkins
Carlsbad, California

Googling
the (OMG venomous!) centipede
in my hand

Carolyn Hall
San Francisco, California

346

she drones on
about writing from the heart
the hard conference chairs

Charles Trumbull
Santa Fe, New Mexico

rolling hills—
wheat pennies in the jar
on my father's desk

Cherie Hunter Day
Cupertino, California

threadbare
in the knot
my emergency tie

David G. Lanoue
New Orleans, Louisiana

Rubbing words, like silk,
between my fingers. Smooth, soft,
stronger than they look.

Deborah Edler Brown
Los Angeles, California

home again
after a week on the road
plum blossoms

Deborah P Kolodji
Temple City, California

summer moon—
out of darkness
a leaf

Diana Ming Jeong
Pasadena, California

the rock
thinking about rolling,
rolling . . .

Don Baird
Palmdale, California

after sunset
    sometimes the clouds light up
let's wait and see

Don Eulert
Santa Ysabel, California

prison concert—
the harpist peering out
through the strings

Don McLeod
Sherman Oaks, California

rust on my driveway
blends with HOA hues
yet I get letters

Elizabeth Williams
San Luis Rey, California

wet sand—
the stork's legs
twice as long

Ellen Cooper
Montréal, Québec

at the edge of the sea entering the barely there

Eve Luckring
Los Angeles, California

summer stars
a travel-sized
Aladdin's Lamp

Fay Aoyagi
San Francisco, California

a dry spring breeze
shakes the old yucca flowers—
rain on my roof

Frank C. Carey
Santa Fe, New Mexico

Tin sunset
the toy robot
walks off the table

Garry Gay
Santa Rosa, California

facing the wind
fading words
on the sign

Gary Hotham
Scaggsville, Maryland

the potato peeler on the table
pointing to him—
life is sometimes quiet

Gene Myers
Rockaway, New Jersey

raw oysters
she remembers
her first time

Genie Nakano
Hawthorne, California

in pine shade
a mother and daughter talk
Boy Scout camp

Gregory Longenecker
Pasadena, California

Graceland
50 shades
of Elvis

Haiku Elvis (Carlos Colón)
Shreveport, Louisiana

no alarm
feathered friends
breaking fast

James Won
Temple City, California

jacaranda petals
stain the sidewalk
first love

Janis Albright Lukstein
Rancho Palos Verdes, California

dry riverbed
too late to say
sorry

Jennifer Sutherland
Glen Waverley, Australia

pink buds of crab apple tree
as big as the later fruit

Jim Applegate
Roswell, New Mexico

the crickets stop chirping that much dawn

Jim Kacian
Winchester, Virginia

autumn chill
dialing her dead mother's number
by mistake

Joan Prefontaine
Cottonwood, Arizona

snow has made a coffin of a stone bench

John Stevenson
Nassau, New York

lotus buds
the glint of pennies
in the fountain

Joshua Gage
Cleveland, Ohio

composted key
does it open a world
on the other side

Kath Abela Wilson
Pasadena, California

produce aisle
a child listens
to the melons

Kathe L. Palka
Flemington, New Jersey

white sea foam
abandoned at high tide
stretch marks

Kathy Fulton
Westminster, California

testing the hotness
of the iron
        spring rain

                        Kimberly Esser
                        Los Angeles, California

they can tie the knot
after all
those years in the closet

                        kris moon
                        Kanagawa, Japan

in my dream
I touch the moon
and it is real

                        Lidia Rozmus
                        Vernon Hills, New Jersey

beach house—
the scent of sunscreen
in an unmade bed

                        Linda M. Papanicolaou
                        Palo Alto, California

piano fugue—
Glen Gould's
twenty fingers

Luce Pelletier
Saint-Basile-le-Grand, Québec

summer moonlight . . .
stretching the strings
of a violin

Makoto Nakanishi
Matsuyama, Japan

after the divorce
she shoots his heirloom china
with his heirloom gun

Marcyn Del Clements
Claremont, California

clouds,
where there is no mountain
a mountain

Margaret Beverland
Katikati, New Zealand

branding time
the sun-tanned 'V'
on the cowhand's neck

Margaret Chula
Portland, Oregon

in Aoyama
an avenue of cherry trees
the other world

Mariko Kitakubo
Tokyo, Japan

another test
for glaucoma
I steal a magazine

Marilyn Shoemaker Hazelton
Allentown, Pennsylvania

a hand sticking out
from the balcony below . . .
small rain

> Michael Dylan Welch
> Sammamish, Washington

where other trees
reach upwards
the willow

> Michael Rehling
> Presque Isle, Michigan

a deer path peters
out in the periwinkle
morning moonset

> Michele Root-Bernstein
> East Lansing, Michigan

buoy bells . . .
her plan to forget one man
with another

Naia
Temecula, California

maple leaf
fan
summer breeze

N. E. Taylor
Los Angeles, California

massaging the dog eyes closed

Oleg Kagan
Los Angeles, California

arriving late—
the others' footprints
snow-filled

Pamela Cooper
Montréal, Québec

frost-covered car
now some drama
in my life

Patrick Gallagher
San Francisco, California

windfall apple
a few geese that should
have moved on

paul m.
Bristol, Rhode Island

new grass
three horses shimmy
in the sand wallow

Paul MacNeil
Ocala, Florida

holiday cards
the connections that survive
those that don't

Peggy Heinrich
Santa Cruz, California

so sweet, this
unripe plum warmed
by your hand

Penny Harter
Mays Landing, New Jersey

old year, new year
somewhere a hospital call bell
beeping and beeping

pjm
San Jose, California

at sunset memory feathers weighed against a cheek

Richard Gilbert
Kumamoto, Japan

winter of divorce
my son pulls apart
the fake white tree

Roberta Beary
Bethesda, Maryland

cheap highway motel
voice of the semi
penetrating rock and wall

Robert Forsythe
Annandale, Virginia

an emerald lagoon
colorful fish swim around
eating each other

Robert Lundy
Del Mar, California

distant party
a bush moth's wings beat
on the porch light

Ron C. Moss
Leslie Vale, Australia

wind from the south
her finger traces the character
for snow

Sandra Simpson
Tauranga, New Zealand

old hunting knife—
in the blood groove a trickle
of pear juice

Scott Mason
Chappaqua, New York

the living room
now looking less lived-in—
spring cleaning

Sean Carlton
West Hollywood, California

summer evening—
a slip of moonlight
between her thighs

Seretta Martin
San Diego, California

cello music
the hotel room
feels warmer

Sheila Sondik
Bellingham, Washington

cedar rain—
all the hope
in mother's chest

Sondra J. Byrnes
South Bend, Indiana

loneliness—
the coffee
lukewarm

Stanford M. Forrester
Windsor, Connecticut

Sparrows flit by.
Even the sick child
  finds a smile.

Steven Carter
Menlo Park, California

wilderness trail
that one moment
I felt lost

Stevie Strang
Laguna Niguel, California

a moment of peace . . .
her children's distant
shouting

Stewart C. Baker
Rancho Palos Verdes, California

curriculum vitae
the years
that went missing

Susan Antolin
Walnut Creek, California

boys hoot their leaps into the blue placid

Susan Diridoni
Kensington, California

fine champagne,
wine and words
are better sipped

Susan Galletti Campion
Spring Valley, California

almost within reach
from the open bus window
tempting persimmon

Susan Rogers
Los Angeles, California

a doe . . .
the path through the forest
in her eyes

Ted van Zutphen
Healdsburg, California

summer dream
the earring maker's hands
on my neck

Terry Ann Carter
Victoria, British Columbia

pelicans
    with nobody in charge
shift into glide

Ute Jamrozy
San Diego, California

cloudy half moon
their last daughter
moves out

Victor P. Gendrano
Seal Beach, California

with all its body
side-to-side over sand dunes
the tongue of god

Victor Ortiz
San Pedro, California

sin after sin
I kill mosquitoes
during meditation

Vuong Pham
Brisbane, Australia

the trail switchbacks up
through the forest
slug's pace

Wakako Miya Rollinger
Topanga, California

fall twilight
in the bungalow for rent
a vacuum sings

William Hart
Montrose, California

Budding cherry
let's forget the formalities
and get started

Yu Chang
Schenectady, New York

First Times

by Deborah P Kolodji

> raw oysters
> she remembers
> her first time

It is said that raw oysters are aphrodisiacs and that Casanova, the famous eighteenth-century lover, used to breakfast each morning on fifty oysters. Indeed, researchers have found that bivalve mollusks, like oysters, are rich in amino acids that trigger increased levels of sex hormones. Even if I hadn't read of this connection, this poem by Genie Nakano, of Hawthorne, California, is rich in unstated sensuality with the juxtaposition of "raw oysters" to "her first time." The nakedness of the oyster subconsciously invokes an image of human nakedness. In addition, there is something about "first times" that resonates with the reader—whether it is the first time for raw oysters, the first time for sex, or another first time in a person's life. We have all had firsts of various sorts: first drinks, first times to ride a bike or drive a car, first times to be betrayed. Some of these firsts are wonderful but others are as awkward as eating a raw oyster, where we might hesitate and find the consistency of the oyster difficult to swallow. We may not like the salty, briny taste, or perhaps find the oysters to be too gritty if not cleaned thoroughly.

We don't know for sure who "her" is—we might assume it is the author. However, I prefer the way this poem sounds in the third person versus the first person because of the assonance between "her" and "remember" and "oyster." Alliteration with "s" and "r" sounds as well as the assonance adds to the poem's musical quality. I ate my first raw oysters in a bar on Catalina Island, so for me this poem evokes the 2013 Haiku North America conference because of our trip to Catalina at the end of the conference.

ONCE UPON A TIME

2015

Michael Dylan Welch and Scott Mason, editors

October 14–18, 2015, 94 anthology contributors, one poem each

Conference Location:
Union College, Schenectady, New York

Haiku North America celebrates its twenty-fifth year with a focus on haiku in education. Perhaps we who write haiku are always perpetual learners, our eyes always wide with wonder at the world around us, at what we can record and share through haiku poetry. And perhaps every haiku is a way of starting a story . . . once upon a time.

All excuses spent,
I tell my wife
about my alien abduction.

Alan Pizzarelli
Bloomfield, New Jersey

Morning glory
twirling around
my little finger

Alexis Rotella
Arnold, Maryland

fading into
a film-noir background
familiar trees

Angela Terry
Lake Forest Park, Washington

rooftop restaurant
a crow drinks up clouds
from an empty table

Angelee Deodhar
Chandigarh, India

anniversary
the entomologist buys the roses
with aphids

Anita Krumins
Toronto, Ontario

winter apples
she thinks
he's a keeper

Anne Elise Burgevin
Pennsylvania Furnace, Pennsylvania

cherry blossoms
she tries on her first
wedding ring

Aubrie Cox
Knoxville, Tennessee

dust devil—
the roadrunner
takes a bath

Barbara Hay
Ponca City, Oklahoma

from flip-flops
to paisley socks
fall term

Beverly Acuff Momoi
Mountain View, California

cranberry sunrise oh to be a bog turtle

Bill Cooper
Midlothian, Virginia

a cigarette smolders
in the cake plate
marathon bingo

Bill Deegan
Mahwah, New Jersey

slow dancing
I pretend
I remember

Bill Kenney
Whitestone, New York

I think I'll build a hut
right here
with these words

Bill Porter / Red Pine
Port Townsend, Washington

sundown
closing both latches
of the compost bin

Brad Bennett
Arlington, Massachusetts

f(ailing)s

Bruce H. Feingold
Berkeley, California

going rogue
I count
my syllables

Carlos Colón
Shreveport, Louisiana

summer birthday caked in sand and sea salt

Carol Ann Palomba
Wanaque, New Jersey

monastery garden
hooded juncos come
to beg for crumbs

Charles Trumbull
Santa Fe, New Mexico

秋風に浮世の塵を払けり

akikaze ni ukiyo no chiri o haraikeri

Tagami Kikusha

dust of an uncertain world
brushed away
by the autumn wind

Cheryl Crowley, translator
Atlanta, Georgia

washed up on shore
the bones
of what we were trying to say

Claudia Coutu Radmore
Carleton Place, Ontario

tiny fruit fly
flying around in circles
aren't you dizzy?

Cynthia Quevedo
Weston, Vermont

open sky yoga
waiting for the key
to get in

Deb Koen
Rochester, New York

taps . . .
all we could say
now said

Deborah P Kolodji
Temple City, California

at the road's edge
a falcon turns
one eye missing

Donna Beaver
Bloomfield, New Jersey

midnight
the ocean moves
the moon

Don Wentworth
Pittsburgh, Pennsylvania

autumn evening
leaves on the steps
outside my door

Edward J. Rielly
Westbrook, Maine

chimes grace chilled air
where pilgrims mount minster steps
Nob Hill Thanksgiving

Elizabeth Williams
Oceanside, California

moonlight
leaves sing
a cappella

Fay Aoyagi
San Francisco, California

dew point—
the words come
after I walk away

Francine Banwarth
Dubuque, Iowa

Cracks and pops
of an old record
autumn colors

Garry Gay
Santa Rosa, California

patches of snow taking longer
our road over
Roman roads

Gary Hotham
Scaggsville, Maryland

dusk
shadows leaving
their bodies

George Swede
Toronto, Ontario

dad's long blessing
rolling off his heaped platter
the turkey leg

Guy Simser
Kanata, Ontario

sound of a stream
in the wind
poplar leaves

Hilary Tann
Schuylerville, New York

tall window
of a ruined church—
the glory of lichens

Ion Codrescu
Constanta, Romania

fever pitch
of coyotes in the darkness
distracts me from the news

Janis Albright Lukstein
Rancho Palos Verdes, California

rivergum walk
magpies warble
at morning recess

Jennifer Sutherland
Viewbank, Australia

grandpa's Victrola
after a wind up
Caruso's clown cries

Jerome Cushman
Victor, New York

fireworks
another swig
of cucumber water

Jessica Tremblay
Burnaby, British Columbia

the vast west
railroad cars decouple
in the dark

Jim Kacian
Winchester, Virginia

sleepless
a summer night
dabbling in rain

John Stevenson
Nassau, New York

The class sits in silence,
captive audience
to the radiator's hiss.

Jonathan Roman
Yonkers, New York

a nun's collection
of nesting glass hens
late-autumn sun

Joyce Clement
Bristol, Connecticut

at the roundabout
a blind snowman
points the way home

Julie Bloss Kelsey
Germantown, Maryland

meadow deer . . .
the slow nibbling away
of daylight

Julie Warther
Dover, Ohio

temple redone
   Kali's tongue
not so red

Kala Ramesh
Pune, India

Hiroshima Day
shakuhachi cracks
at every node

Kath Abela Wilson
Pasadena, California

Valentine's Day
park pigeons settle on
LO
VE

Kathe L. Palka
Flemington, New Jersey

the one I love
sitting out back
with the feral cats

Lee Gurga
Lincoln, Illinois

polished wood shelf
the book collection
doubled

Leena Luther
Albany, New York

film over budget
the color of snow
is negotiable

LeRoy Gorman
Napanee, Ontario

back home
on garbage day
the womanizer

Luce Pelletier
Saint-Bruno-de-Montarville, Québec

crunching
spring cabbages
hippopotamus

Makoto Nakanishi
Matsuyama, Japan

depression
each snowflake
apparently different

Marco Fraticelli
Pointe Claire, Québec

terror forgotten
she licks the hand that bathed her
toyger kitten

Marcyn Del Clements
Claremont, California

positive . . .
magnolia buds
browned by frost

Marietta Jane McGregor
Canberra, Australia

wind flower—
how calm the color
of cloud before dusk

Marilyn Shoemaker Hazelton
Allentown, Pennsylvania

abandoned quarry
standing at the bottom
an inukshuk

Maxianne Berger
Outremont, Québec

autumn dusk
the Van Gogh
in the sunflowers

Meik Blöttenberger
Hanover, Pennsylvania

first frost
a retelling
of the fable

Melissa Allen
Madison, Wisconsin

pumpkin weigh-in . . .
the judge's motion
to lift off hands

Michael Dylan Welch
Sammamish, Washington

big shot
the olives
in his martini

Michael Ketchek
Rochester, New York

trail map
you are here
and now

Michele Root-Bernstein
East Lansing, Michigan

open sky—
a kite pinned in place
by the wind

mychael zulauf
Baltimore, Maryland

salvation army
buying back my donated
stilettos

Pamela A. Babusci
Rochester, New York

supermoon—
they abandon
their selfie sticks

Pamela Cooper
Montréal, Québec

iced tea with lemon
an undeclared contest
for best grandmother

Patrick Gallagher
Pacific Grove, California

a coyote disappears
    down the deer track
        burst milkweed pods

paul m.
Bristol, Rhode Island

dusting the mantel
my feeling stone smoothed
on an ancient shore

Paul W. MacNeil
Ocala, Florida

balsa wood gliders
powered by rubber bands
early evening tryout

Peg McAulay Byrd
Madison, New Jersey

mother's pastry brush—
stiff bristles bending
more each year

Penny Harter
Mays Landing, New Jersey

morning walk
how the gulls have grown
to ignore me

Peter Newton
Winchendon, Massachusetts

winter's bone the smell of sushi

Philip Rowland
Tokyo, Japan

kayak conversation
the blue heron
hears enough

Randy M. Brooks
Taylorville, Illinois

autumn arrives
cool breeze stretches
the harbor's mooring lines

Richard Schnell
Keeseville, New York

only their cawing
in the snowstorm
visible

Rick Black
Arlington, Virginia

spring
the first drop of rain
wets a beetle's back

Rob Dingman
Herkimer, New York

at the top
of the ferris wheel
mary jane

Roberta Beary
Bethesda, Maryland

home early
I explain my lay-off
to the dog

Robert Forsythe
Annandale, Virginia

shoes off, coat in tray
belt removed, pockets emptied
I feel so secure

> Robert Lundy
> Del Mar, California

dark winter river
in the shallows a splash
of vibrant sunset

> Ruth Yarrow
> Ithaca, New York

eddy pool
the dream becomes
                clear

> Scott Glander
> Glenview, Illinois

conch to my ear sonic boom

> Scott Mason
> Chappaqua, New York

tangled lives—
i square the placemat
with the table

Sondra Byrnes
Santa Fe, New Mexico

Year of the Sheep—
another month
wanders off

Stanford M. Forrester
Windsor, Connecticut

late apology—
the parted beak
of a carved bird

Susan Antolin
Walnut Creek, California

mall Santa—
when I sit on his lap
he ho ho ho's

Susan Burch
Hagerstown, Maryland

dawn's chorus the sisters at lauds

Susan Diridoni
Kensington, California

old poet's reading
each book dedicated
to a new woman

Terry Ann Carter
Victoria, British Columbia

once upon a time
on grandma's porch
the world

Tom Clausen
Ithaca, New York

deep winter
a painted lady asleep
in the firewood

Tom Painting
Atlanta, Georgia

brigadoon morning
a squirrel upside down
on the bird feeder

Wanda D. Cook
Hadley, Massachusetts

each year
they get more prominent
my bunions

Wonja Brucker
Duanesburg, New York

cotyledon
there is always
a cry

Yu Chang
Schenectady, New York

morning meditation
    hummingbird visits
        the prayer flags

Zoanne Schnell
Keeseville, New York

An Immense Sky

by Tom Clausen

the one I love
sitting out back
with the feral cats

The complexion of human relationships involves seemingly endless revelations and new or renewed understandings. To be in love with someone , especially in a long-term relationship, requires devotion and sacrifice that is at once selfless and compassionate. As Rilke suggests in his book, *Letters to a Young Poet*:

> The point of marriage is not to create a quick commonality by tearing down all boundaries; on the contrary, a good marriage is one in which each partner appoints the other to be the guardian of his solitude, and thus they show each other the greatest possible trust. A merging of two people is an impossibility, and where it seems to exist, it is a hemming-in, a mutual consent that robs one party or both parties of their fullest freedom and development. But once the realization is accepted that even between the closest people infinite distances exist, a marvelous living side-by-side can grow up for them, if they succeed in loving the expanse between them, which gives them the possibility of always seeing each other as a whole and before an immense sky.

In this haunting haiku by Lee Gurga, of Lincoln, Illinois, the opening line inspires wonder at what we know about this "one." The second line gives the poem a sense of distance, which may at first be unsettling. The season may be summer or at least an agreeable time of year to be sitting outside. As with many successful haiku, the third line is a surprise in how it hints at the poet's relationship with his loved one. As much as people in a relationship give nurture, comfort, and provide balance and stability to each other, they can also oppress, dominate, and wear each other out through too much sustained closeness. The best relationships are an art form where each partner divines when the other partner needs space, and how much. This poem recognizes one of those moments.

We can also feel a touch of humor, as if the poet were allowing, at times, that his loved one might prefer the company of feral cats rather than his own. The poem seems to ask, "How could the one I love be sitting out back when I'm right here?" And perhaps the poet's partner wishes for a bit more wildness in their relationship, as suggested by the fact that these cats are feral. Whatever the case, we see compassion in this poem—the partner's compassion for the cats, and the poet's compassion for his partner, a love and admiration that runs deeper because of recognizing the partner's compassion and giving it the space it needs. Through it all, as readers, we may feel compassion not just for this domestic moment, but even for haiku itself, because of its ability to see in this way. Lee Gurga's poem is indeed about love, respect, and space, and an understanding that relationships center on acceptance. As Rilke said, "Love consists of this: two solitudes that meet, protect, and greet each other."

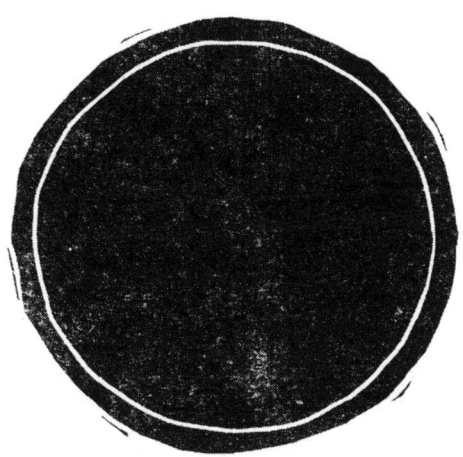

HNA CONFERENCES
AND ORGANIZERS

August 23–25, 1991
Las Positas College, Livermore, California
Directors: Garry Gay, Michael Dylan Welch, Jerry Ball, David Wright,
Christopher Herold, and Paul O. Williams

July 15–18, 1993
Las Positas College, Livermore, California
Directors: Garry Gay, Michael Dylan Welch, Jerry Ball, David Wright,
Ebba Story, and Marianne Monaco

July 13–15, 1995
Ryerson Polytechnic University, Toronto, Ontario
Directors: Keith Southard, Marshall Hryciuk, and George Swede

July 24–27, 1997
Portland State University, Portland, Oregon
Directors: Ce Rosenow, Margaret Chula, and Cherie Hunter Day

July 8–11, 1999
Northwestern University, Evanston, Illinois
Directors: Charles Trumbull, Sara Brant, Joseph Kirschner, and Lidia Rozmus

June 28–July 1, 2001
Boston Conservatory, Boston, Massachusetts
Directors: Raffael de Gruttola, Judson Evans, and Karen Klein

June 26–29, 2003
Dalton School, New York, New York
Directors: Pamela Miller Ness, Stanford M. Forrester, Brenda Gannam,
Tom Painting, and John Stevenson

September 21–25, 2005
Fort Worden Conference Center, Port Townsend, Washington
Directors: Michael Dylan Welch, Christopher Herold, Carol O'Dell,
and Doris Thurston

August 15–19, 2007
Hawthorne Inn and Conference Center, Winston-Salem, North Carolina
Directors: Dave Russo, Lenard D. Moore, and Bob Moyer

August 5–9, 2009
National Library of Canada, Ottawa, Ontario
Directors: Terry Ann Carter, Guy Simser, and Claudia Radmore

August 3–7, 2011
Seattle Center, Seattle, Washington
Directors: Michael Dylan Welch, Tanya McDonald, and Angela Terry

August 14–18, 2013
Queen Mary, Long Beach, California
Directors: Deborah P Kolodji and Naia

October 14–18, 2015
Union College, Schenectady, New York
Directors: Hilary Tann, John Stevenson, Yu Chang, Tom Clausen,
and David Giacalone

CONTRIBUTORS

This index accounts for about 540 unique contributors of poetry and commentary to this anthology, including poets such as Bashō, Buson, Shiki, and a few others whose poems have been translated.

Printed in Great Britain
by Amazon